Pantry & Preservation

Cooking from Scratch, Learning from Scratch

By Maggie Smarr

Pantry & Preservation

Copyright © 2025 by Maggie Smarr.

All rights reserved. No part of this book may be reproduced in any form or by any electronic or mechanical means, including information storage and retrieval systems, without permission in writing from the publisher, except by reviewers, who may quote brief passages in a review.

This publication contains the opinions and ideas of its author. It is intended to provide helpful and informative material on the subjects addressed in the publication. The author and publisher specifically disclaim all responsibility for any liability, loss, or risk, personal or otherwise, which is incurred as a consequence, directly or indirectly, of the use and application of any of the contents of this book.

MILTON & HUGO L.L.C.
4407 Park Ave., Suite 5
Union City, NJ 07087, USA

Website:	www. miltonandhugo.com
Hotline:	1- 888-778-0033
Email:	info@miltonandhugo.com

Ordering Information:
Quantity sales. Special discounts are available on quantity purchases by corporations, associations, and others. For details, contact the publisher at the address above.

Library of Congress Control Number:	2025906645	
ISBN-13:	979-8-89285-513-6	[Paperback Edition]
	979-8-89285-512-9	[Digital Edition]

Rev. date: 04/14/2025

TABLE OF CONTENTS

MEALS FOR THE WHOLE FAMILY 1
- Lasagna & Pasta Shells 2
  - *Giant Pasta Shells* 2
- Elk Meatloaf 3
- Elk Burgers & Buns 4
- Potstickers 5
- Loaded Country skillet 6
- Gyros 7
- Roast 8
- One Pot Greek Soup 9
- Greek kabobs & Terriyaki kabobs 10
- Chicken Nuggets & Chicken strips 11
- Chicken Pot Pie 12
  - *Pie Crust* 12
- Chicken Enchiladas 13
  - *Red Enchilada Sauce* 13
- Tamales 14
- Chicken Chili & Cornbread 15
- Chicken Taco stir fry 16
- Stir Fried rice 17
  - *Chicken Ginger Stir fry* 17
- Whole roasted Chicken 18
- Chicken & Dumpling Soup 19
- Chicken & Gnocchi Soup 20
  - *Gnocchi* 20
- Oven Parmesan chicken 21
  - *Creamy Skillet chicken (Italian Dish)* 21
- Lemon baked salmon & terriyaki salmon 22
- Smoked & Canned Salmon 23
- Fish Tacos 24
  - *Drizzle Salsa* 24
- Beer Batter mix/Fried Fish 25
- Gnocchi & homemade pasta 26
  - *Universal Pasta recipe* 26

BREAKFAST ... 27
- Biscuits & Gravy ... 28
- Buttermilk Pancakes & Same-day Sausage ... 29
- Basic Crepes ... 30
  - *Easy French Toast* ... 30
- Quick Cinnamon Rolls ... 31
  - *Cream Cheese Icing* ... 31
- Sourdough cinnamon rolls ... 32
- Sourdough Danishes ... 33
- Breakfast Casserole ... 34

SIDE DISHES ... 35
- Cilantro Lime Rice ... 36
  - *Spanish Red Rice* ... 36
- Mac & Cheese ... 37
  - *Calico Baked Beans* ... 37
- Green Bean Casserole ... 38
- Straight Guacamole ... 39
- Mexican Corn Salad ... 40
  - *Hot Corn Dip* ... 40
- Mango Pico De gallo ... 41
  - *Mild Homemade salsa (water bath canned)* ... 41
- Greek Salad & Vinaigrette ... 42
  - *Sweet Cabbage Salad* ... 42
- Deviled eggs ... 43
- Marinated Carrots ... 44
  - *Tomato Soup* ... 44
- Hibachi/Miso Soup ... 45
- Sauerkraut / Kimchi ... 46

DESSERTS ... 47
- Chocolate chip cookies (OG) ... 48
  - *White Raspberry Cookies* ... 48
  - *Peanut Butter Cookies* ... 48
- Cookies (Orange, Lemon & Sugar) ... 49
- Whoopie pies ... 50
  - *Molasses Cookies* ... 50
- Apple Pie & Pie crust ... 51
- Apple Crisp ... 52
  - *Homemade Ice cream (no churn needed)* ... 52
- Banana Bread ... 53
  - *Zucchini Cinnamon Swirl Bread* ... 53
- Donuts/Maple Bars ... 54
- Brownies (Healthy vs fudgy) ... 55

- *Easy Fudgy brownies (9x9 pan)* 55
- Cheesecake & soft caramels 56
- Chocolate & vanilla cake 57
  - *Vanilla Cake (2 cake round pans)* 57
- Carrot "Spice" Cake 58
- Blackberry Cobbler Cake 59
- Lemon Blueberry Muffins 60
  - *Lemon Bars (9x13 casserole dish)* 60
- Gummies/Fruit Leathers 61
- Yogurt & Drinks 62
  - *Yogurt drinks* 62
- Bars (Chickpea & Granola) 63
- Discard crackers/cereal 64
  - *Cereal/graham crackers* 64
- Creamer, Syrup, Marshmallows 65

BREADS 66
- Gyro/Pita bread 67
  - *Tortilla (16 tortiillas)* 67
- Cheesy Drop Biscuits 68
  - *Buttermilk biscuits* 68
- Hawaiian/Dinner Rolls 69
- Sandwich Bread 70
- Sourdough bread (artisan) 71
- Sourdough Baguettes 72
- Sourdough Bagels 73
- Pizza dough/sour-pizza-do 74
  - *Large Sourdough flat pizza* 74
- GLUTON FREE FAVORITES 75
  - *Cinnamon Rolls* 75

FRIDGE & PANTRY FROM SCRATCH 76
- Sourdough Starter 77
- Kombucha 78
  - *SCOBY RECIPE* 78
- Apple Cider Vinegar/White vinegar 79
  - *Other Vinegar* 79
- Farm Cheddar cheese 80
- Soft Cheeses 81
  - *Mozzerella* 81
  - *Ricotta/cottage cheese* 81
  - *Cream cheese* 81
- Sauces 82
  - *Alfredo* 82

- *Pizza* 82
- *Pasta* 82
- *Tomato sauce* 82

Other Sauces 83
- *Terriyaki* 83
- *Tzatziki* 83
- *Soy sauce* 83

Condiments 84
- *Ketchup* 84
- *BBQ* 84
- *Mayo* 84
- *Mustard* 84
- *Sour Cream* 84

Homemade Seasoning 85
- *Italian* 85
- *Taco* 85
- *Buillion* 85
- *Ranch* 85

Homemade Extract & Rennet 86
- *Vanilla* 86
- *Maple* 86
- *Lemon* 86
- *Mint* 86
- *RENNET* 86

Maple Syrup & Eggnog 87
- *Eggnog* 87
- *Maple Syrup OG & Taste-a-like* 87

Homemade Chocolate 88
- *White chocolate* 88
- *Milk chocolate* 88
- *Semisweet* 88
- *Dark chocolate* 88

Jam 89
- *White chocolate* 89
- *Blackberry* 89
- *Strawberry (6 cups)* 89
- *Grape* 89

Icing/frosting 90
- *Cream cheese icing* 90
- *Royal icing* 90
- *Buttercream* 90
- *Ganache* 90

Bone/Veggie/Chicken broth 91
- *Chicken broth (8 cups)* 91
- *Bone broth* 91

- *Veggie* 91
- General Canning Tips 92
  - *Waterbath* 92
  - *Pressure Canning* 93
- General Dehydration Tips 94
  - *Herbs* 94
  - *Veggies* 94
  - *Fruit* 94
  - *Liquids* 94
  - *Meat* 94
- Meat Preservation Tips 95
  - *Cold Smoking* 95
  - *Hot Smoking* 95
  - *Freezing* 96
- Substituting Made Easy 97

MEALS FOR THE WHOLE FAMILY

PANTRY & PRESERVATION 1

LASAGNA & PASTA SHELLS

• 9x12 pan   • Freezer Friendly

INGREDIENTS

1 lb Ground meat

¾ lb Ground sausage meat

1 Spaghetti packet (3 tbsp of seasoning) [see pg __ for recipe]

1 large Can of tomato sauce (29 oz)

1 Can of tomato paste (6 oz)

½ cup Mozzarella cheese

1 cup Parmesan cheese

8 oz of Ricotta cheese

1 box lasagna noodles

1 tsp salt

INSTRUCTIONS

1. Brown the meat in a skillet.
2. Add the spaghetti packet and tomato sauce into the skillet, stir until bubbling.
3. Add parmesan cheese. Set aside/remove heat.
4. Boil lasagna noodles in a separate pot with a pinch of salt then strain after time listed on the box.
5. Laye your 9x13 casserole dish in this order: Meat sauce, noodle, Ricotta and repeat x3.
6. Bake in the oven at 350 for 1 hr. in the last 10 minutes add a thin layer of mozzarella cheese

GIANT PASTA SHELLS

INGREDIENTS

1 box pasta shells

15 oz ricotta cheese

1 cup parmesan cheese

1 cup mozzerralla cheese

1 egg

2 tsp dried parsley

1 tsp basil

1 tsp salt & pepper

1 16 oz can of pasta sauce

INSTRUCTIONS

1. Preheat oven to 350.
2. Boil giant pasta shells in a large pot for 8-10 minutes, strain/cover.
3. In a large bowl mix ricotta, mozzerrela, parmesion, eggs, parsely, salt and pepper.
4. Fill shells with the cheesy filling, and place into a casserole dish.
5. Pour jar of pasta overtop all of the pasta shells.
6. Bake at 350 for 35-60 minutes.

NOTE: If making ravioli/homemade pasta the above recipe is a great filling for any pasta type.

ELK MEATLOAF

- Requires a read Pan
- Freezer Friendly

INGREDIENTS

1 ½ lb ground meat

2 eggs

1 can tomato sauce (15 oz)

1 med yellow onion (finely chopped)

1 cup bread crumbs

1 ½ tsp salt

⅛ tsp pepper

(GLAZE)

3 tbsp brown sugar

3 tbsp dijon mustard

3 tbsp apple cider vinegar

INSTRUCTIONS

1. Beat eggs, add tomato sauce, onion, crumbs, salt/pepper, mix well.
2. Add in meat and mix by hand
3. Press into bread pan
4. Small bowl mix glaze ingredients.
5. Pour glaze overtop
6. Bake uncovered for 70 min at 350.

PANTRY & PRESERVATION

ELK BURGERS & BUNS

• 1 lb = 6 burgers   • 10 buns

INGREDIENTS

Salt

Pepper

1 Egg (if fat content <20%)

1 ½ lbs ground meat (elk is best)

(BUNS)

3 Cups Flour

3 Tbsp sugar

2 ¼ tsp instant yeast

1 ½ tsp salt

1 cup warm water (110*)

1 lg egg

3 Tbsp butter

GLAZE/COLORING

1 egg yolk/1tbsp water

Pinch of sesame seeds

INSTRUCTIONS

1. Add egg to meat if needed and mix well. Form into ½ in thick meat patties.
2. Generously salt/pepper them.
3. Grill until thoroughly browned, approx 4-5 minutes on each side in Traeger/grill at 400-500 degrees

(BUNS)

1. Mix sugar, yeast, water allow sit for a few minutes until frothy.
2. Mix in flour, salt, then beat in egg, butter.
3. Knead 3-5 min (or dough hook). Transfer to an oiled bowl for 1 hr. rise.
4. Punch down, divided into 10 balls, flatten each slightly 2-3 in diameter.
5. Cover/rise 30-45 min.
6. Brush with egg wash/sesame seeds and bake for 13-16 min at 350 degrees.

(Can freeze buns for later)

POTSTICKERS

- (Ground meat-elk/turkey/deer)
- Freezer Friendly

INGREDIENTS

(FILLING)

1 lb ground meat

1 tsp ginger

2 cloves garlic

1 cup shredded carrots

1-2 shredded Zuchini

1 bunch scallionsw

1 tsp red pepper flakes

1 tbsp soy sauce

½ tsp salt

¼ tsp pepper

(WRAPPER)

2 ½ cup flour

¼ tsp salt

⅔ cup hot water

⅓ cup cold water

5 tbsp oil for frying

Soy sauce for dipping

INSTRUCTIONS

(DOUGH WRAPPER)

1. Mix flour salt, hot water by hand, then add in cold water, kneading for 1 min.
2. Let rest in fridge for 30 min.
3. Roll out dough and cut to shape. (I cut into squares)

(FILLING)

1. Cook/brown ground meat with seasoning and set aside.
2. Cook carrots/zucchini until soft then add back in meat, and top with scallions. Pour into large bowl. (you can blend for finer texture here if preferred)
3. In deep skillet/pot add oil for frying.
4. Add filling into dough, pinch edges into the center and fry about 2 min or until golden brown on both sides.

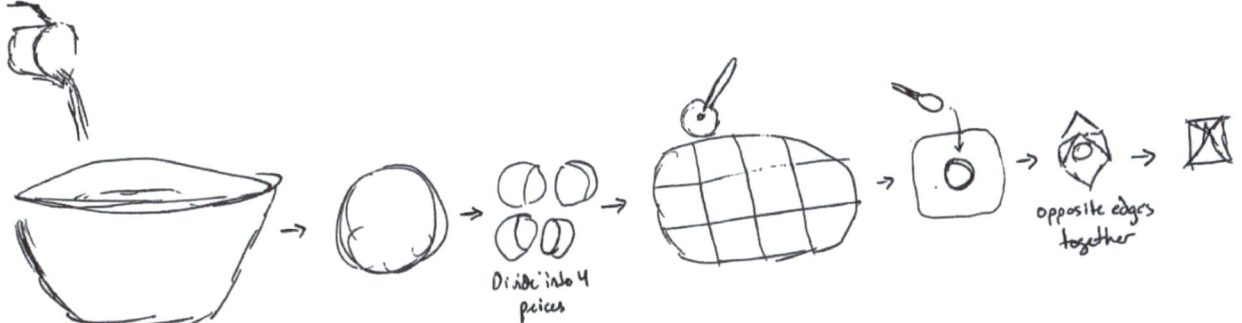

LOADED COUNTRY SKILLET

INGREDIENTS

1.5 lb ground meat (elk, deer, cow, etc)

2 cloves garlic

2 bell peppers (diced)

2 tomatoes (diced)

4 potatoes (cubed)

1 yellow onion (diced)

1 large bunch of spinach or kale

1 tsp Salt & pepper

1 tsp red pepper flakes

2 tsp cumin

1 Bunch green onions (chopped)

1 tbsp Worcestershire sauce

1 tbsp Balsamic vinegar

1 tbsp olive oil.

INSTRUCTIONS

1. Add oil, meat, cumin salt/pepper and cook through until browned. Set ASIDE

2. Parboil diced potatoes in a small pot for 3 min, then remove and pat dry.

   Add oil and potatoes to the skillet, cook until golden, do NOT stir too often. Let sit and flip for approx. 20 min. Set ASIDE

3. Add oil, bell pepper, onion, garlic to skillet cooking approx. 6 min or until lightly caramelized.

4. Add tomatoes, spinach/kale for another 3-5 min.

5. Pour in the balsamic and Worcestershire sauce

6. Add back in the meat and potatoes mix well and top with green onions.

PANTRY & PRESERVATION

GYROS

• (Great with deer meat)

INGREDIENTS

2 lbs lamb/deer ground meat

½ cup red onion diced

2 tbsp Italian seasoning

2 tsp salt

1 ½ tsp garlic powder

½ tsp black pepper.

TOPPING

1 cup diced tomatoes

1 cup shaved lettuce

½ cup sliced red onion

½ cup crumbled feta

1 cup tzatziki sauce

(see pg _83___ for sauce recipe)

See Pg_67_ for gyro/Pita bread recipe.

INSTRUCTIONS

1. In a large bowl combine meat, spices, and fine red onion.

2. **For strips** of meat bake in a bread pan at 400 degrees for 30-35 minutes.

    OR

    For a quicker meal, toss all those ingredients into a skillet and cook until thoroughly browned.

3. In a medium bowl add the ingredients listed as topping to the left, cut/dice as stated.

4. Slice your gyro's and fill with your meat and top with your toppings.

Optional: Squeeze lemon wedges on top if desired.

ROAST
• (Requires a slow cooker)

INGREDIENTS

3 lb chuck roast

(or deer/elk roast)

Pinch salt/pepper

1 tbsp oil

1 yellow onion

5 garlic cloves

2 tsp Worcestershire sauce

1 tbsp thyme

1 tbsp rosemary

2-3 lb whole small potatoes

5 medium carrots (chunks)

1 ¼ cup beef broth

2 tbsp fresh parsley

INSTRUCTIONS

1. Pat dry the roast then cover & rub with salt/pepper
2. Sear meat in skillet (about 2-4 min each side)
3. Place in slow cooker
4. Add oil, onion, garlic to skillet & sauté (about 2 min) then pour over roast In crockpot.
5. Layer carrots/potatoes over roast salt and pepper as desired.
6. Add broth, Worcestershire, thyme, rosemary into skillet or small saucepan and heat for about a minute.
7. Pour broth mixture over everything.
8. Cook in crockpot 8-9 hours on low.

ONE POT GREEK SOUP

INGREDIENTS

1 tbsp oil or butter

1 yellow onion (diced)

½ lb of cauliflower florets

1-2 bell peppers(chopped)

2 lbs chicken breast(whole)

1 ½ tsp paprika (or more)

1 tsp oregano

1 ½ tsp salt

½ tsp pepper

4-8 cups of chicken broth

(Add broth until ingredients are covered)

1 cup chopped spinach

¾ cup feta

8 oz cream cheese

1 lemon (juiced)

INSTRUCTIONS

1. Sauté onions & garlic in butter/oil in large pot.
2. Add cauliflower, bell pepper, and whole chicken breast, cover in seasoning. Lastly add broth until the ingredients are covered.
3. Bring broth to boil, then simmer and cover for 10-15 min

    {NOTE: until chicken reaches temp of 165}
4. Remove chicken & shred it, return to pot
5. Add feta, spinach, cream cheese, lemon juice & simmer another 5-10 min.
6. Eat with Pita Bread (YUM). (See pg _67_ for pita bread recipe).

GREEK KABOBS & TERRIYAKI KABOBS

INGREDIENTS

2 lb chicken breast

½ cup plain Greek yogurt

4 cloves garlic

¼ cup olive oil

1 tsp lemon zest

3 tbsp lemon juice

2 tbsp red wine vinegar

1 ½ tsp oregano

½ tsp paprika

1 ½ tsp salt

½ pepper

6 oz Crumbled feta

Group of chopped parsley`

Tzatziki sauce

INSTRUCTIONS

1. cut chicken into 1 inch pieces, place in Ziploc or dish and set aside.
2. in a bowl mix Greek yogurt, garlic, olive oil, lemon zest, lemon juice, red wine vinegar, oregano, paprika, salt, pepper.
3. Pour mixture into the Ziploc of chicken, marinate for 30 minutes-up to 4 hours.
4. soak wooden skewers for moist chicken.
5. Grill until thoroughly cooked for about 10 minutes. Or Place in warmed skillet, Leaving the meat to sear, and turning occasionally for about 20-30 min. (until meat reaches 165).

TERRIYAKI KABOBS

INGREDIENTS

1 can or fresh pineapple

1 purple onion

2 lb chicken

(thighs are the most flavorful)

Terriyaki sauce of choice

(or go to pg _83_)

Kabob sticks

INSTRUCTIONS

1. Cut chicken into medium size chunks.
2. Marinade chicken in teriyaki sauce for about 30 minutes
3. Cut up onion skin into big enough squares to be placed on kabab stick.
4. Preheat Smoker/BBQ/Treager to 400 degrees
5. Prep kabobs with chicken, onion, pinapple, etc.
6. Cook on BBQ for about 20 min & enjoy.

CHICKEN NUGGETS & CHICKEN STRIPS

• Freezer Friendly

INGREDIENTS

1 lb ground chicken

(or use meat grinder w/ chicken breast)

3 tbsp of milk

1 slice of bread (or ¼ cup breadcrumbs)

¾ tsp garlic salt

1/8 tsp pepper

1 egg

3 tbsp melted butter

BREADING

1 cup of breadcrumbs

¼ cup parmesan cheese

2 tsp dried parsley

INSTRUCTIONS

1. Preheat oven to 375
2. Add bread and milk to a bowl and let sit until absorbed. Then add garlic and salt/black pepper. Mix well.
3. Use a meat grinder or food processor to shred the chicken meat. Add mixture before using your hands to thoroughly combine meat and seasoning.
4. shape the mix into nugget shapes and set aside.
5. Add the breading ingredients into a bowl, and mix. (if using a slice of bread, toast until very crunchy and run through a grinder/food processor to create bread crumbs.)
6. In a new small bowl add one egg, mix well.
7. Dunk the chicken nuggets into egg mix then the breading.
8. Brush/spray with melted butter or oil.
9. Bake for 7 min, flip/spray with butter or oil. And bake another 8 minutes.

CHICKEN STRIPS

INGREDIENTS

Salt/pepper

2 eggs

1-2 cups of flour

Breading

2 full chicken breasts

(Can add any seasoning desired)

Ex. Paprika, garlic, johnny's, etc.

INSTRUCTIONS

1. Get out 3 small bowls and prepare a sheet tray with grates & nonstick material.
2. In one bowl add flour/salt pepper & desired seasonings. In second bowl add the 2 eggs (lightly beat to blend in yolk). In the third bowl add in breading with desired seasoning.
3. Cut chicken into desired size strips.
4. Pat the chicken dry then coat with flour, then egg, ending with the breading.
5. Evenly space strips on sheet pan & cook at 375 for 20 min. (or until meat reaches 165 degrees).

CHICKEN POT PIE

- (This makes x2 pies) • Freezer Friendly

INGREDIENTS

1 lb. chicken cubed

1 cup of pea

1 cup of carrots

1 onion

1 cup of celery

1 tsp salt

½ tsp pepper

1 cup milk

1/3 cup of butter

½ cup flour

2 cups of chicken broth

Optional: I add green beans and lima beans, sometimes I use zucchini peeled and diced instead of celery. You can use a variety of veggies, so mix it up.

{NOTE: if frozen cook 30 min covered, 30 min. uncovered}

INSTRUCTIONS

1. Cook chicken with salt/pepper & *set aside.*
2. Sauté butter, onions, carrots, celery in large skillet (5-10 min).
3. sprinkle in flour slowly and stir until smooth, cook for about 1 minute.
4. Add broth & milk, stir constantly until mixture is thick and bubbly (~10 min).
5. Stir in chicken and precooked peas, carrots (or other desired veggies).
6. Remove from heat and let the mixture begin to cool off.
7. Prepare 1 pie crust into a pie dish. Pour Meat filling into pie dish, then layer the 2nd pie crust over top pinching the edges of dough together. I use a fork to imprint a nice pattern.
8. Cut 4 incisions into top of pie for venting (& decoration). Then cover with tinfoil.
9. Cook at 30 min covered with tinfoil at 400 then uncovered for 15 minutes in the oven.

PIE CRUST

INGREDIENTS

2 ½ cups flour

½ tsp salt

1 cup chilled butter

½ cup cold water

This makes 4 medium circles for pie.

INSTRUCTIONS

1. Add flour and salt into large bowl.
2. Cut cold butter into small cubes and drop into the flour.
3. Using a butter cutter, masher, or a fork mix butter into four until crumbly
4. Add water by tbsp and mix thoroughly until dough-like. I form the ball by hand. Cover dough in saranwrap and let rest in fridge for 30-60 min.
5. Cut into 4 pieces, roll out one lay over pie dish, fill with filling, roll out second and cover filling. Repeat with 2nd pie.

CHICKEN ENCHILADAS

- (9x12 casserole)
- Freezer Friendly

INGREDIENTS

2 tbsp oil

1 small yellow onion

1 ½ lb. of chicken (cubed or shredded)

1 can diced green chillis (or fresh)

1 tsp of salt

1 tsp pepper

1 can black beans

2 cups of cheddar cheese

1 cup cottage cheese

1 batch red enchilada sauce

1 bag of tortilla shells

INSTRUCTIONS

1. In a large skillet sauté onions/oil/chicken until golden brown, then add in the green chilis (~6-10 min)
2. Add black beans & turn off the heat.
3. Pour a small amount of red sauce on the bottom of the casserole dish and spread.
4. Assemble tortillas in this order.

    Ched. Cheese → Chicken/beans → 1 tbsp red sauce → cheddar cheese → 1 tbsp cottage cheese
5. Fold & roll placing seam side down in casserole dish. See image.
6. Pour any remaining red sauce and cheddar cheese on the tops of all the enchiladas.
7. Cook uncovered 20 min @ 350

RED ENCHILADA SAUCE

INGREDIENTS

1 tbsp oil

1 tbsp flour

1/8 cup chili powder

¼ tsp garlic

¼ tsp cumin

¼ tsp oregano

1 cup chicken broth

INSTRUCTIONS

Small pot, and low heat stir seasoning in oil until pasty.

Add flour last

Pour in broth slowly, whisk until completely combined

Bring to boil then simmer for 10 min.

PANTRY & PRESERVATION

TAMALES

INGREDIENTS

1 package of dried corn husks

6 cups masa

2 tsp salt

2 tsp cumin

1 tsp baking powder

6 cups of chicken broth

3-4 cup oil (olive, avocado)

1 cup salsa

2-3 cups of precooked shredded chicken

4 oz of red sauce (see pg 16)

+ another 4 oz for later

½ cup of cheese.

NOTE: Good in the fridge for 3 days in an airtight container, freeze whole for up to 3 months. For reheating add water to container to help keep tamale moist.

After removing the husk cover the tamale with cheese and a red sauce to soak into the masa right before eating.

INSTRUCTIONS

1. Soak the corn husks in a large pot of warm water until soft.

2. In a large bowl (use mixer if you have it), combine masa, salt, cumin, and baking powder. Beat in oil on low, pouring in the chicken broth slowly. Then increase the speed to medium/high for 10 minutes.

3. Once fluffy, cover with a wet cloth and place in your fridge until it's time to use.

4. Prepare your filling. I use my instant pot and cook my chicken breast for 12 minutes, then shred it. Add red sauce and a cup of salsa. Mix well. (Make sure the filling is not too wet)

5. Lay out the corn husk, Place 1-2 large spoonsful of the masa, spread lightly with wet fingers.

6. Add a small spoonful in the center of the masa, fold the husk in half so that the masa touches itself like a taco. Then peel back one side of the husk and roll the husk so that the taco shaped masa has been tucked under.

7. On the skinnier side of the corn husk fold it upwards and tie it with a ripped up corn husk. See image.

8. In large steamer pot, place the corn husks upright and steam for 30 min.

14 PANTRY & PRESERVATION

CHICKEN CHILI & CORNBREAD

- (Large family size serving)

INGREDIENTS

2 lbs chicken

1 onion

2 cans diced green chilis

1 can salsa

32 oz v8 juice

2 cans kidney beans

2 cans black beans

2 cans corn

2 packets taco seasoning

1-2 tbsp cumin

{can alternatively use ground meat, by cooking in same steps as listed above)

INSTRUCTIONS

1. Sauté & cook chicken and onion in a large pot.
2. Add seasoning, then chilis, salsa, and v8 juice. Stir until bubbling

    {OPTIONAL: can add diced tomatoes, bell peppers, etc. if wanted.)
3. Rinse beans out of the can and add to pot. Then add the corn last.
4. Cover, bringing to a boil, then dropping the heat to a simmer for 20 minutes.
5. Crunch tortilla chips into your soup bowls & enjoy! (see page 67 for tortilla recipe)

NOTE: If starting with raw beans, soak overnight in water, then Boil for 1-2 hours (larger beans up to 3 hours)

CORN BREAD

INGREDIENTS

2 cups of flour

1 ½ cup cornmeal

2 ½ cup milk

¾ cup sugar

2 eggs

1 stick of butter

1 tsp salt

1 tbsp baking powder

INSTRUCTIONS

Pregrease a 9x13 casserole dish with butter.

In a medium bowl combine milk, cornmeal, butter, and eggs.

In a large bowl (or mixer) combine the flour, baking powder, sugar, and salt. Then pour in the liquids from the previous bowl. Mix well then pour into casserole dish & bake for about 30 minutes.

Heat 3 tbsp butter with 3 tbsp honey to pour overtop after it's done baking.

CHICKEN TACO STIR FRY

• Freezer Friendly

INGREDIENTS

1 lb. of chicken

1 yellow onion

2-3 bell peppers

3 cloves garlic

1 tbsp oil

1 tbsp cumin

3 tbsp taco seasoning

½ cup light beer (or water)

Add red peppers/chili powder for more spice.
Add lime or tajin for more sourness.
Replace water with beer for more savory

INSTRUCTIONS

1. Cut onions into strips, not diced. Cut bell pepper into strips. And cut chicken into strips.
2. Cook chicken in oil on a skillet.
3. Once thoroughly brown add onions, bell peppers, garlic. Cook another 3-5 minutes, then pour in seasoning, and water
4. Cover and simmer for about 10 min.
5. Serve as is in tacos or top with additional flavorings like lime, cilantro, etc.

See page _67_ for tortilla recipe.

STIR FRIED RICE

INGREDIENTS

1 lb chicken (cubed very small)

1 tbsp garlic powder

2 tbsp soy sauce

1 tbsp oil

1 tbsp siracha sauce

3-5 eggs

1-2 cups rice (precooked)

3 tbsp soy sauce

3 tbsp sesame oil

+

1 frozen bag mixed carrots/peas or canned mixed carrots/peas. Or fresh precooked carrots/peas (1 cup carrots:1 cup peas)

INSTRUCTIONS

1. Dice, then season chicken with garlic, and siracha by hand.
2. Cook chicken via skillet then set aside
3. Cook/thaw veggies then push to the side of the skillet.
4. Pour in pre-beaten eggs, cook until fully scrambled.
5. Dump in rice, pour in soy sauce and sesame oil.
6. Add back in chicken and mix!

CHICKEN GINGER STIR FRY

INGREDIENTS

1 lb chicken

2 tbsp cornstarch

½ tsp garlic powder

½ tsp ground ginger

2 tbsp sesame oil

1 tbsp olive oil

1 zucchini (half moon diced)

1-2 carrots (match sticks diced)

¼ cup soy sauce

2 scallions (green onions)

INSTRUCTIONS

1. chop chicken & coat it by hand in cornstarch garlic & ginger
2. Using 1 bsp of olive oil and 1 tbsp of sesame oil in skillet cook the chicken 6-10 min until golden.
3. Add in soy sauce then set aside.
4. Add in 1 tbsp sesame oil to skillet, then cook zucchini and carrots. (3-5 min).
5. Add back in chicken.
6. Top with green onions.

PANTRY & PRESERVATION

WHOLE ROASTED CHICKEN
• (Requires large Dutch oven)

INGREDIENTS

1 Whole Chicken

VEGGIE BED

4 potatoes

3-6 carrots

1 yellow onion

1 lemon(quartered)

Olive oil

Salt/Pepper

1 tsp rosemary

1 tsp thyme

HERBED BUTTER

1 stick butter

5 garlic cloves (minced)

1 tsp rosemary

2 tsp thyme

1 zest of a lemon

2 tsp salt

½ tsp pepper

CHICKEN INSIDES

½ yellow onion

1 lemon quartered

Sprinkled rosemary/thyme

INSTRUCTIONS

1. 1.. Thaw if frozen, in the fridge night/day before (approx. 24 hours).

2. 2. Layer bottom of Dutch oven with veggie bed. Half the potatoes, diced onion and carrots.

3. 3. Remove what the innards from the chicken then replace with the "chicken insides".

4. 4. Find the chicken breasts and lightly loosen the skin from the breast. Push half the herbed butter solution into the pocket between breast and skin.

5. 5. Pat the skin as dry as possible, then cover the skin in the remaining herbed butter.

6. 6. Place whole chicken into Dutch oven, pull wings under chicken, keep the breast side up. Tie legs if necessary.

7. 7. Cook covered in oven @425 for 1 hr and 30 min. Then uncovered for 30 min.

{NOTE Cook approx. 20 min per pound of chicken, you want to reach 165 degrees)

CHICKEN & DUMPLING SOUP

• (Requires large pot/ Dutch oven)

INGREDIENTS

DUMPLINGS

1 cup flour

1 egg beaten

2 tsp baking powder

½ tsp salt

2 tbsp green onion(chives)

½ cup buttermilk

SOUP

Precooked chicken

2-3 stalks celery

2-3 large carrots

1 yellow onion

4-8 cups of chicken broth

½ stick butter

½ tsp thyme & rosemary

1 tsp pepper.

NOTE: add chicken broth as needed or water/ bouillon ration of 1 cup:1 tsp

INSTRUCTIONS

1. In a medium bowl whisk dough ingredients together (Don't overmix). Set it aside.
2. Sauté butter & onions in large pot, shortly after adding in rest of veggies.
3. Add broth, seasoning and meat.
4. Bring the pot to boil.
5. Drop tbsp size Dumpling dough mix into the boiling soup.
6. Cover and bring down the heat to a simmer for 20 min.

CHICKEN & GNOCCHI SOUP

• (Similar to Olive garden)

INGREDIENTS

3 tbsp olive oil (or butter)

1 large yelow onion

1 cup shredded carrots

2 stalks celery diced

4 cloves of minced garlic

1 ½ tsp salt

½ tsp pepper

4-6 cups of chicken broth

2 cups chicken

(shredded and cooked)

1 tbsp thyme leaves

1 lb of potato gnocchi

2 large handfuls of spinach

1 ½ cup of half and half

INSTRUCTIONS

1. Heat 3 tbsp oil in a Dutch oven/large pot.
2. Add chopped onion, carrots, celery, garlic, salt, and pepper in. Stir until slightly golden (~5 min)
3. Stir in chicken broth, shredded chicken and fresh thyme. Bring to boil.
4. Reduce to simmer for 10 minutes.
5. Add gnocchi, spinach, and half and half to pot.
6. Cook until all gnocchi appear to float, and spinach is wilted.

(If using frozen gnocchi-add gnocchi at the boiling step 3).

NOTE: add chicken broth as needed or water/bouillon ration of 1 cup:1 tsp

---

GNOCCHI

INGREDIENTS

1 large potato

1 egg

1 cup flour

1 tsp salt

½ tsp pepper

Optional: Garlic, onion powder, alternative seasoning/flavors add by ½ tsp.

NOTE: I use leftover mashed potatoes or potato soup often to make gnocchi at later dates. Add flour or water to get correct consistency if doing this approach.

INSTRUCTIONS

1. Peel and cut up 1-2 potatoes, and place in a small pot of boiling water. Keep on med/high for about 15-20 minutes or until you can poke through the potato easily.
2. Strain potatoes and mash well (use a food mill or potato ricer for best results, no chunks is best).
3. In a large bowl combine the potatoes, egg, flour, salt, and seasonings. Stir/knead until dough like.
4. Divide the dough into 4 pieces. With the first piece start rolling into a long snake/worm shape on a clean surface, add flour as necessary to prevent sticking. Once it's to the thickness of a pinky finger, use a knife or flat edge spatula to cut into ½ inch increments. Lightly flour and set aside. Repeat with 3 other pieces of dough.
5. Use for the above recipe, or by itself in boiling water for 1-2 minutes (until floating). You can also freeze for later.

OVEN PARMESAN CHICKEN

• Freezer Friendly

INGREDIENTS

2 lb. chicken breast

2-3 tbs olive oil

¼ cup grated parm

½ tsp paprika

½ tsp garlic powder

½ tsp onion powder

½ tsp chili powder

½ tsp oregano

½ cup fresh shredded parm

INSTRUCTIONS

1. Cut chicken into desired strip size. I recommend cutting the chicken thickness in half. So, the strips are thin.
2. One bowl fill with fresh shredded parm.
3. Second bowl add olive oil and seasoning.
4. Dip chicken into the seasoning bowl then parm before placing it into a large casserole dish.
5. Cook in oven at 400 for about 15-17 min. (until chicken reaches 165).

CREAMY SKILLET CHICKEN (ITALIAN DISH)

INGREDIENTS

2 tbsp olive oil

1 lb. chicken (cubed)

1 tsp Italian seasoning

½ tsp salt

½ tsp pepper

4 cloves garlic

1 cup sundried or diced tomatoes

3 cups broccoli florets

½-1 cup chicken broth

½-1 block cream cheese

or cup of heavy cream.

INSTRUCTIONS

1. Cook chicken in oil, add in salt/pepper/Italian seasoning.
2. Add in garlic, tomatoes, broccoli, chicken broth, bring to a light boil. Stir for the first few minutes then cover and bring down to a simmer for about 10 minutes.
3. stir in cream & simmer for about 5 more minutes.
4. Serve with spaghetti noodles or rice.

PANTRY & PRESERVATION

LEMON BAKED SALMON & TERRIYAKI SALMON

• Freezer Friendly

INGREDIENTS

1 Salmon

~Spread~

4 garlic cloves

1 tbsp dijon mustard

2 tbsp honey

1 tsp lemon zest

¼ tsp paprika

¼ tsp basil

1/8 tsp red pepper flakes

1/8 tsp pepper

1-2 tsp salt.

INSTRUCTIONS

1. mix ingredients in bowl.
2. Place salmon on tinfoil and apply spread to top of salmon.
3. add/cover and seal with tinfoil, sealing the edges.
4. Cook covered for 10-14 min at 400.
   Ensure it has reached 145 degrees internally
5. Broil uncovered for 2-3 minutes.

TERRIYAKI SALMON (OVEN BAKED)

INGREDIENTS

1 Salmon

3 Tbsp butter

1 tsp salt/pepper

1 cup terriyaki sauce

INSTRUCTIONS

Do steps 1-4, then add teriyaki sauce in last 5 min for broiling. SERVE with Mango pico de gyo on Pg __41__ for best results!

SMOKED & CANNED SALMON

• Smoked

INGREDIENTS

1 Salmon

4 cups of water

1 cup brown sugar

1/3 cup course kosher salt

BASTING FLUID

Honey/Maple syrup as needed

INSTRUCTIONS

1. Brine/soak salmon in brown sugar, salt/water for 12+ hrs covered in a casserole dish or Large ziplock.
2. Smoke at 165 for 2 ½ - 3 ½ hrs
3. BASTE with maple honey mix at least once an hour while smoking.

CANNED SALMON/CHICKEN

INGREDIENTS

1 Salmon or chicken

½ tsp vinegar (per jar)

1 pinch salt (per jar)

INSTRUCTIONS

1. Cut salmon into bite size pieces (deboned, no scales). Fill clean jars (leave 1 inch before rim).
2. Add seasoning/preferred spices, wipe the rims to ensure theyre dry. Place on lids.
3. Pressure can at about 10 lbs of pressure for 1 hour (half pint), 75 minutes (pints).

NOTE: Your elevation matters, psi and time may change based on your elevation (above recipe is for sea level 1000 feet of less.

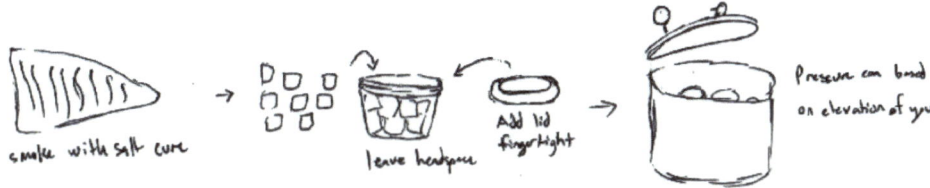

FISH TACOS
• (Oven baked)

INGREDIENTS

1 lb of white fish

½ cup flour

1 ½ tsp chili powder

1 tsp salt

½ tsp pepper

½ cup milk

1 tbsp butter

¼ cup oil for frying!

INSTRUCTIONS

1. Cut the fish across the grain into ½ in wide and 3 inch long pieces
2. Add the fish into a bowl of milk, and preheat the skillet of frying oil.
3. In a new bowl combine flour, chili, salt, and pepper.
4. Dip fish into the seasoning bowl and then add to the skillet to fry.
5. Cook 3-4 min, turn and cook for 1 more minute.

{NOTE: Fish needs a temperature of 145 internally}

DRIZZLE SALSA

INGREDIENTS

¼ cup mayo

½ cup sour cream

(or plain greek yogurt)

½ tsp salt/pepper

½ lime

¼ purple onion

1 clove garlic

2 tomatoes diced

½ cup cilantro

½ jalepeno (no seeds)

INSTRUCTIONS

1. Dice up the tomatoes, onion, cilantro and jalapenos.
2. Mix wet ingredients and seasoning.
3. Pour the mixture on top of the veggies.
4. Eat as a side or on top of your taco!

*NOTE: Amazing on all tacos but especially street tacos.

Tortilla recipe on pg 67

BEER BATTER MIX/FRIED FISH

• (Frying batter)

INGREDIENTS

1 tsp salt

½ tsp pepper

2 tsp seasoned salt

1 cup flour

1 tbsp garlic powder

1 tbsp paprika

1 egg (beaten)

1 1/3 cup light beer

1 bottle of frying oil.

INSTRUCTIONS

1. Add frying oil to a deep pot, reach a depth of approx. 2-3 inches.
2. Heat oil in a pot to 375 degrees.
3. Pat content dry (fish, veggies, chicken, cheese, etc.)
4. In a medium bowl whisk the ingredients together, adding the beer last.
5. Dip contents into batter and quickly but carefully place into the fry oil.
6. Cook approx. 3-4 min. flipping halfway through if necessary.

{NOTE: To keep pieces warm, place them in the oven warm setting while you finish the rest of what your frying.}

GNOCCHI & HOMEMADE PASTA

• Freezer Friendly

INGREDIENTS

GNOCCHI

1 cup mashed potato

1 egg

½ tsp salt

½ tsp pepper

¼ tsp garlic powder

¼ tsp onion powder

1 cup flour

INSTRUCTIONS

1. Boil 2-3 potatoes, run through a ricer or immersion blender until smooth. Let cool potatoes cool.
2. Add all the ingredients together, kneading until texture feels like dough.
3. Section out the dough and use your hands roll until it's about the width and shape of a finger. Then cut the log into little squares.
4. Repeat until all the dough is cut into tiny squares (add flour to prevent sticking).
5. 5. Take a fork, then push down and pull the fork towards you on the squares to make the wavy texture. Then use or freeze. Boil until floating. (~2 minutes

---

UNIVERSAL PASTA RECIPE.

INGREDIENTS

1 egg

1 cup flour

½ tsp salt

See page 2 for a cheesy filling recipe & pg. 84 for sauce recipe

INSTRUCTIONS

1. Create flour volcano, add eggs to center.
2. Mix until its dough (~5 min) by hand or dough hook in a mixer.
3. Cut the dough into 4 pieces and roll until thin. Cover extra dough with wet towel to keep moist.
4. Lightly dust the dough to prevent sticking, fold it into itself 3 times and cut into strips according to your desired size.

   OR

   You can use pasta maker for finer slices, spaghetti shaped noodles, or to roll out large pieces to be filled with cheeses/meats for ravioli.

5. Cook by boiling water, then add the pasta for approximately 2-3 minutes for egg noodles, 7 minutes for ravioli, 8-10 min for spaghetti.
6. Otherwise freeze or hang dry until hard and keep in airtight container.

BREAKFAST

BISCUITS & GRAVY

• Freezer Friendly

INGREDIENTS

BISCUITS

2 1/2 cups flour

2 tbsp baking powder

2 tsp honey

1 tsp salt

½ cup butter(cold & cubed)

1 cup of buttermilk

GRAVY

2-3 Tbsp butter

½ lb ground sausage

(or ½ lb ground meat, highly seasoned with Italian herbs).

¼ cup flour

2 ½ cup milk.

Salt/pepper

NOTE: You can make buttermilk at home with this ratio

Whole milk 1 cup:1tbsp vinegar

INSTRUCTIONS

BISCUITS

1. Cut butter into flour in a large bowl. Until the flour appears crumbly.
2. Add all other dry ingredients and stir.
3. Gradually add in the cold buttermilk,
4. Combine until like dough.
5. pat/roll dough into a rectangle and fold into thirds. Repeat these 2 more times. (refrigerate as needed to prevent butter from melting too much).
6. Use a small bowl/cookie cutter to cut out the biscuits (don't twist, only press)
7. Arrange biscuits on a cookie sheet, brush them with leftover buttermilk and bake it for 15-17 min at 425

GRAVY

1. Heat Sausage in skillet until fully cooked in butter.
2. stir in flour until well combined cooking for another minute.
3. Slowly whisk in the milk until gravy thickens boils. Then reduce heat to a simmer for 2-4 minutes.
4. Pour over your biscuits!

28 PANTRY & PRESERVATION

BUTTERMILK PANCAKES & SAME-DAY SAUSAGE

• Freezer Friendly

INGREDIENTS

1 Cup flour

1 large egg

1 cup buttermilk

1 tsp baking soda

½ tsp salt

1 tbsp sugar.

1 Tbsp melted butter

NOTE: You can make buttermilk at home with this ratio

Whole milk 1 cup:1tbsp vinegar

For Buttermilk Waffles just add one more tsp of baking soda. Then Cook in a waffle iron (about 2 minutes)

INSTRUCTIONS

1. Add all dry ingredients into bowl.
2. Add in egg, and slowly add/mix in buttermilk.
3. Try not to overmix, but try to break down any flour chunks.
4. Add the melted butter at the end and mix lightly.
5. Use ¼ cup of the batter to pour over a preheated griddle (to 350) for dollar sized pancakes.
6. Flip pancakes when bubbles begin to form/pop.

SAME DAY SAUSAGE

INGREDIENTS

½-1 lb of ground meat (elk, deer, turkey, beef)

1 egg

½ tsp pepper

1 tsp salt

1-2 tbsp italian seasoning (oregano, thyme, basil)

INSTRUCTIONS

1. In a large bowl combine all ingredients by hand.
2. Form meat into small patties or link shapes and place into a preheated skillet.
3. Cook until thoroughly browned.

BASIC CREPES

• Freezer Friendly

INGREDIENTS

1 cup flour

2 Eggs

½ cup milk

½ cup water

½ tsp salt.

Optional: *I like to add 1 tbsp of flax seeds to make it easier for spreading the batter and increased nutrient value*

INSTRUCTIONS

1. Whisk ingredients until very smooth consistency. Adding the melted butter last.

2. Using a ¼ cup of the batter, pour over a preheated griddle (to 350 degrees), using the bottom of the metal cup to smooth out/spread the batter very thin on the griddle.

3. Flip as soon as the batter appears somewhat "dry" (approximately 1-2 minutes) then cook another minute or until lightly browned.

NOTE: Add fruit, powdered sugar, whipped cream, maple syrup as desired for filling

---

EASY FRENCH TOAST

INGREDIENTS

6 slices of bread

2 eggs

½ cup of milk

¼ tsp vanilla extract

½ tsp cinnamon

½ tsp white sugar

INSTRUCTIONS

1. Find a flat/wide enough casserole dish or bowl to fit a slice of toast and use it to beat the eggs, add milk, vanilla, cinnamon, and sugar. Mix until bubbly.

2. Soak both sides of each slice of toast before placing into a preheated skillet or griddle to cook until golden brown. (2-4 minutes each side approx)

QUICK CINNAMON ROLLS

• (Pie pan)   • Freezer Friendly

INGREDIENTS

2 cups flour

2 tbsp white sugar

2 tsp baking powder

1 tsp salt

3 tbsp butter

2/3 cup whole milk

FILLING

¼ cup white sugar

¼ cup brown sugar

2 tsp cinnamon

2 tbsp butter

INSTRUCTIONS

1. Add all ingredients together in a large mixing bowl.
2. Roll out dough into a large rectangle
3. Sprinkle filling over rectangle.
4. lightly press filling into dough, then cut into 1-inch-wide strips (9-12 of them)
5. Roll each strip into a cinnamon roll and place into a prebuttered pie pan. Or 8x8 dish.
6. Bake at 400 for 20-25 minutes.
7. Add icing and enjoy!

CREAM CHEESE ICING

½ brick of cream cheese

1-2 tbsp soft butter

1 tsp vanilla extract

½ cup of powdered sugar.

Whisk together in a bowl until smooth.

For better designs place inside a ziplock and cool in fridge for 5 minutes before cutting a corner and "piping" the cinnamon rolls.

SOURDOUGH CINNAMON ROLLS

• (9x12 pan)   • Freezer Friendly

INGREDIENTS

2/3 cup milk

2 tbsp butter

1 egg

½ cup sourdough starter

2 tbsp sugar

2 ½ cups flour

1 tsp salt

FILLING

2 tbsp melted butter

½ cup brown sugar

3 tsp cinnamon

1 tbsp flour

Optional: Add ¼ cup of heavy cream in the last 10 minutes of baking for fluffier/moist rolls.

INSTRUCTIONS

1. Add milk into large bowl, then the sourdough starter mixing well.
2. Mix rest of dough ingredients with dough hook or by hand until dough consistency.
3. Let rest covered in fridge overnight.

    (can keep in a warm area for 6 hrs straight if you want to speed the process)
4. Remove dough from fridge and rest for 30 min.
5. Roll out dough into a cookie sheet sized rectangle
6. Mix filling ingredients in a small bowl then sprinkle/smear over dough.
7. Cut rectangle into 9-12 strips and roll each one into cinnamon roll shape.
8. Place rolls into prebuttered 9x12 baking dish and cover/rise for 1-2 hours or until visibly puffy.
9. Bake 35-40 min at 350.
10. See pg_91__ for icing recipes, but cream cheese icing is my favorite

SOURDOUGH DANISHES

- (x2 cookie sheets) • Freezer Friendly

INGREDIENTS

3 cups flour

¼ cup white sugar

½ cup sourdough starter

3/34 cup milk

1 egg

½ tsp vanilla extract

1 tsp salt

LAYERING WITH

2 sticks of butter

CREAM CHEESE FILLING

3 oz cream cheese

2 tbsp gran sugar

1 egg yolk

½ tsp lemon

½ tsp vanilla extract

NOTE: Can also use Jam for added flavor.

ICING

1 cup powdered sugar

½ tsp vanilla extract

2 tbsp milk

EGG WASH

1 egg

1 tbsp water

INSTRUCTIONS

1. Add the milk and sourdough starter together in large mixer, stir well.

2. Add in the rest of ingredients except butter, and stir, then knead in the mixer for 7 minutes.

3. Let rest covered In a preoiled bowl, in fridge overnight (approx 8-12 hours)

4. Use two parchment sheets to sandwich two softened sticks of butter. Shape the butter into about a 4 x 10 in rectangle. Rest in fridge until cold.

5. Roll out the dough into a larger, cookie sheet sized rectangle.

6. Lay butter in the center of dough, then fold the edges of dough inwards into a three fold. Rest in fridge for 20 minutes.

7. Roll out dough and repeat the trifold. Rest in fridge 20 minutes. Repeat. And Prep cream cheese filling.

8. After Rolling out the dough cut into about 12-14 squares. Separate onto 2 different cookie sheets. Fill with jam & cream cheese filling 1 tbsp worth.

9. Pinch each corner inwards, brush with eggwash and bake at 400 for 15 min. Add icing once cooled.

PANTRY & PRESERVATION

BREAKFAST CASSEROLE
• Freezer Friendly

INGREDIENTS

18 eggs

1 ½ cup of milk

~6 slices of bread

(enough for bottom layer of 9x13 pan)

1 package of bacon (precooked)

1-2 tsp salt/pepper

2 cups of cheese

~OPTIONAL~ (my version)

1/3 diced onion

½ diced bell pepper

3 precooked/cubed potato bites.

INSTRUCTIONS

1. Cook accessory ingredients now/ahead of time such as sausage, bacon, or potatoes (hashbrown).

    (BACON-oven 400 degrees for 20 minutes

    HASHBROWN-Skillet for 20 minutes)

2. Butter a 9x13 dish, layer with ripped apart bread chunks

3. Place a layer of cheese

4. Scatter toppings.

5. In a separate bowl whisk the eggs with milk/salt/pepper.

6. Pour mixture overtop of dish.

7. Bake for 40 min at 375 degrees.

NOTE: you can make mini casserole/egg bites by following all these instructions into a muffin pan. Bake for about 30 minutes at 375.

(freezer friendly)

SIDE DISHES

CILANTRO LIME RICE

• Freezer Friendly

INGREDIENTS

2 cups white rice

2 cloves minced garlic

1 small yellow onion

1 lime & zest

1 bunch of cilantro

1 tsp salt

3 tbsp butter

2 cups of chicken broth

INSTRUCTIONS

1. Sauté butter, garlic and onions in instant pot.
2. Rinse rice until no longer cloudy then also saute in instant pot.
3. add lime zest, and chicken broth into instant pot.
4. Press rice setting (or boil then simmer for 20-30 min).
5. Add lime juice, cilantro, and salt/pepper after fluffy/cooked.

SPANISH RED RICE

INGREDIENTS

2 cups rice

1/8 cup butter

8 oz tomato sauce

6 cilantro

1 tsp salt

1 tsp minced garlic

4 cups chicken broth

¼ tsp cumin

¼ tsp garlic

INSTRUCTIONS

1. Saute rice in the butter, once lightly brown add in broth, tomato sauce, salt, garlic, cumin, into pot.
2. Stir/simmer for 30-40 min on stovetop or use instant pot rice setting.

MAC & CHEESE

• Freezer Friendly

INGREDIENTS

1 box of macaroni elbows

1 stick of butter

4 cups of milk

4 cups sharp cheddar cheese

1 tbsp salt

(1/2 for noodles/1/2 for sauce)

1 tsp pepper

3-5 tbsp sifted flour

INSTRUCTIONS

1. Boil macaroni in pot per box & grease 9x13 dish.
2. melt butter in a saucepan, add 3 cups of milk and salt/pepper until boiling.
3. add in cheese/stir
4. sift in flour slowly/whisk constantly.
5. Add in last cup of milk.
6. Pour macroni noodles into the 9x13 dish, then pour saucepan overtop.
7. Bake for 40-50 min at 375.

CALICO BAKED BEANS

INGREDIENTS

½ lb ground meat

¼ lb (precooked bacon)

1 cup chopped yellow onion

1 can kidney beans

1 can lima beans

1 can of pork & beans

1 tsp vinegar

1/3 cup brown sugar

1 cup BBQ sauce

1 tsp yellow mustard.

INSTRUCTIONS

1. In a skillet brown the meat and drain excess fat. Add onions and caramelizes with the meat.
2. Rinse the lima and kidney beans before adding to the meat mixture. Pour in rest of ingredients.
3. Bake in the oven at 350 for 30 minutes. (Can bake cast iron skillets, but if using other type of skillet, transfer all ingredients to a casserole dish).

GREEN BEAN CASSEROLE

• Freezer Friendly

INGREDIENTS

1 can mushroom condensed soup

½ stick of butter

¾ cups of milk

½ tsp salt

2-3 cans of green beens

(or about 2 lbs of fresh beans)

1 1/3 cups of crispy friend onions

INSTRUCTIONS

1. Preheat the oven to 350 and grease a 9x9 sized dish.
2. Melt the butter, cream, milk in a small pot until bubbling.
3. Put green beans into greased dish.
4. Pour the pot mixture over top the beans. Sprinkle fried onions on top.
5. Space a few pats of butter on the very top.
6. Cook 30-40 min at 350.

STRAIGHT GUACAMOLE

• Freezer Friendly

INGREDIENTS

4-5 avocados

1 purple onion diced

1 red bell pepper diced

1 jalapeno thinly diced

4-5 Roma tomatoes diced

5 limes

2 cloves garlic

1 bunch of cilantros

Pinch of salt/pepper

INSTRUCTIONS

1. Mash avocados in medium sized bowl.
2. Dice up onion, bell pepper, tomatoes, and the jalapeno. Remove jalapeno seeds fully.
3. Mix diced veggies into the mashed avocados, garlic and cilantro.
4. Add lime juice and salt/pepper as desired.

PANTRY & PRESERVATION

MEXICAN CORN SALAD

• Freezer Friendly

INGREDIENTS

4 ears of corn
(or 1 can)
1 garlic clove
1 lime
½ tsp salt
1 can black beans
1 bell pepper
¼-1/2 purple onion
½ cup cilantro diced
¼ cup conjita cheese
(alternatively, parm cheese).

DRIZZLE

½ cup plain Greek yogurt
½ lime
1/tsp honey
½ tsp paprika
¼ tsp cumin.

INSTRUCTIONS

1. Char corn in oil in skillet. Add in garlic to char as well (2-3 min).
2. Remove corn into a medium bowl and add the salt and ½ a lime in. Let Corn Cool.
3. In large bowl mix in the beans (after rinsing), diced onion, bell pepper, cheese, and cilantro.
4. Create the ~DRIZZLE~ in a small bowl, mixing well. Then pour over Corn salad.

NOTE: If starting with raw beans, soak overnight in water, then Boil for 1-2 hours (larger beans up to 3 hours)

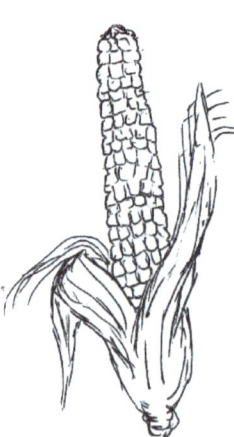

HOT CORN DIP

INGREDIENTS

1 cans of corn
1 tsp cumin
¼ tsp oregano
½ tsp paprika
1 cups shredded pepper jack cheese
1/2 cup shredded parmesion
1 cups mayo
½-1 chopped jalapeno
½ cup of diced green chiles.
3 strips of bacon (diced)

INSTRUCTIONS

1. Precook bacon.
2. Find a pie pan, or 9x9 glass dish, set aside.
3. In a large bowl combine all of the ingredients except the bacon. Fill designated dish. Then sprinkle the bacon on top.
4. Bake at 350 degrees for 25 min.

MANGO PICO DE GALLO

• Freezer Friendly

INGREDIENTS

2 Ripe mangos

2 tomatoes

1 bunch cilantro

½ purple onion

2 cloves garlic

1-2 limes

INSTRUCTIONS

1. Peal mangos and cut around the hardened center. Dice into very small pieces. Put in a medium bowl.

2. Dice and add tomatoes, onion, garlic to bowl. Last in is cilantro.

3. Juice limes into bowl and enjoy.

~TIP~ Tastes delicious with teriyaki salmon recipe.

MILD HOMEMADE SALSA (WATER BATH CANNED)

INGREDIENTS

4 cups of seeded/peeled/cored tomatoes

3 green onions (diced)

1 jalapeno pepper

2 cloves garlic (minced)

1 tbsp lime juice

¼ cup vinegar (5% acidic)

1 tbsp cilantro

1 tsp salt

1 pinch of red pepper flakes

INSTRUCTIONS

1. In a large pot, combine all ingredients and bring to a boil then decrease the heat, you'll simmer the pot for about 15 minutes.

2. Prepare clean jars and pour in ingredients from the pot. (leave at least ½ inch from the top rim)

3. Wipe the rim, place on lid, and then prepare a large pot or water bath canner pot with boiling water. Place in jars (make sure there is 1-2 inches of water above the jars). Boil for about 20 minutes.

4. Remove and rest jars for 24 hours on a towel on your counter.

(If too watery you can always add tomato paste, or simmer the salsa mixture for a longer period)

PANTRY & PRESERVATION

GREEK SALAD & VINAIGRETTE

• **Freezer Friendly**

INGREDIENTS

1 English cucumber
½ red onion
1 red bell pepper
1 yellow bell pepper
1 pint of cherry tomatoes
½ lb of feta cheese (1/2-inch chunks)
½ cup olives pitted

VINIEGRETTE

2 cloves garlic minced
1 tsp oregano
½ tsp Dijon mustard
¼ cup red wine vinegar
1 tsp salt, ½ tsp pepper
½ cup olive oil.

INSTRUCTIONS

1. Peel and remove seeds from cucumber.

   Large dice the bell peppers, and half the cherry tomatoes.

   Thin dice the red onion.

2. Combine all ingredients in a large bowl. Adding the feta and olives last.

3. In a small bowl combine vinaigrette.

4. Pour vinaigrette over veggies and set aside to blend flavors.

5. Serve at room temperature.

NOTE: If out of feta cheese feel free to subsitute with shredded parmesion or mozzaralla.

SWEET CABBAGE SALAD

INGREDIENTS

2 packages of ramen
½ cup sliced almonds
¼ cup sesame seeds
½ cup butter.
1 head of cabbage
1 bunch of green onions
Dressing
1/8 cup white sugar
½ cup olive/avocado oil
¼ cup red wine vinegar
1 tbsp soy sauce.

INSTRUCTIONS

1. Shred the head of cabbage or use a long knife and cut into thin strips.

2. In large bowl add in chopped onions.

3. In medium skilled brown the two packages of ramen noodles broken up in small pieces in butter. Add in almonds, sesame seeds after about 2 minutes, and brown as well.

4. Add cabbage into skillet. Mix thoroughly. Lightly sauté the cabbage.

5. Pour all ingredients back into large bowl.

6. Mix the ingredients in a small bowl and pour over salad.

DEVILED EGGS

INGREDIENTS

6 eggs

½ cup mayo

2 tsp dijon mustard

2 small pickles.

Paprika for dusting

½ tsp salt/pepper

INSTRUCTIONS

1. Bring a pot of water to a boil then remove from heat to add in the eggs. (If using farm fresh eggs, add 1 tbsp of vinegar to boiling water)

2. Boil for about 13-14 minutes.

3. Prepare a medium bowl with ice and water, once eggs are done place into ice water until fully cooled.

4. Peel and cut eggs in half, remove yolks into a medium bowl.

5. In the medium bowl, mash egg yolks, and combine with mayo, mustard, pickles, salt and pepper.

6. Scoop approximately 1 tbsp full of mixture on to each egg half. Dust with paprika.

MARINATED CARROTS

• (8-10 servings)   • Freezer Friendly

INGREDIENTS

2 lbs of carrots

1 large yellow onion

1 large green bell pepper

1 can Campbells tomato soup

¾ cup sugar

¼ cup oil

¾ cup vinegar

1 tsp salt

1 tsp black pepper.

INSTRUCTIONS

1. Peel carrots and cut into rounds. Sliice onion strips and cut bell pepper into chunks.
2. In a medium pot cook the carrots until tender (about 5-7 minutes of boiling).
3. Drain carrots and cool.
4. In a saucepan combine soup, sugar, vinegar, salt and pepper. Bring to boil and stir until the sugar has dissolved.
5. Place carrots, bell pepper, and onion slices in a 10x10 shallow pan or close equivalent.
6. Pour sauce over the carrots, cover and chill.

TOMATO SOUP

INGREDIENTS

1 onion

½ stick of butter

2 cups of chicken or veggie broth

½ tsp salt and pepper

5 tomatoes

4 cloves of garlic

INSTRUCTIONS

1. Cut onion and tomatoes in half, place garlic and bake in oven at 400 for 15 minutes.
2. Pour ingredients into large pot and add the broth, and melted butter. Heat to medium, light bubble.
3. Use an emersion blender until smooth or place in blender/food processor.
4. For smoother consistency use a food mill or a sift and large spoon over another bowl and sift out skins/seeds.

HIBACHI/MISO SOUP

• Freezer Friendly

INGREDIENTS

1 container of mushrooms (thinly sliced)

4 cups of beef broth

1-2 tsp sesame oil

4 cups chicken broth

1 cup carrots (chunks)

1 tbsp ginger sliced

4 green onions

INSTRUCTIONS

1. In a large pot, sauté the onion, garlic, carrots, and ginger in the pot with the sesame oil. Lightly caramelize.

2. Pour in chicken and beef broth and bring to a boil. Then lower to a simmer for at least 1 hour.

3. Scoop out vegatables from pot, and add in the mushrooms and scallions, bring to a light boil then remove from heat.

4. Add in salt/pepper as desired.

NOTE: Miso tastes better the longer it cooks, feel free to use crock pot or on stovetop on low, to simmer broth up to 12-16 hours if you wish.

SAUERKRAUT / KIMCHI

INGREDIENTS

KIMCHI

1 medium napa cabbage head (2 lb)

¼ cup kosher salt

6 cloves garlic (minced)

1 tsp ginger (grated)

1 tsp granulated sugar

2 tbsp fish sauce (or 3 tbsp water)

1-5 tbsp gochutgaru (Korean red pepper flakes)

8 oz radish into matchsticks

1 carrot into matchsticks.

4 medium scallions chopped.

INSTRUCTIONS

1. Cut the cabbage long ways into 4 pieces, remove the cores, then slash each one in 2 inch wide strips.

2. In a large bowl over the cabbage in salt, rubbing it into the leaves, then cover all the cabbage in water. Weigh down the cabbage, for 1-2 hours in the water.

3. Drain out the water and thoroughly rinse the cabbage (get all that salt out!), set aside. Combine all the seasoning, use gochutgaru based on spiciness preference.(1-5).

4. Squeeze out excess water from cabbage and combine with paste thoroughly (use gloves).

5. Pack into jars, let the brine juice cover the cabbage., seal the jar & ferment 1-5 days (place jars in a large box/catch overflow). Store in fridge when done.

SAUERKRAUT

INGREDIENTS

½ cup vinegar

½ cup sugar

½ cup + 2 tbsp pickling salt

1 gallon water.

3 cabbages.

Optional: pinch of red pepper.

INSTRUCTIONS

1. In large pot boil the vinegar, sugar, salt, and water. Stir until sugar/salt dissolve.

2. Rinse off cabbage and cut to fit into mason jars aligned on/in a large cardboard box.

3. Pour hot mixture over top of cabbage in the jars. (add in red pepper currently if desired).

4. Stir lightly, and cover with lids & place in a warm space for 3 weeks to ferment. Eat or store for later.

DESSERTS

CHOCOLATE CHIP COOKIES (OG)

• Freezer Friendly

INGREDIENTS

2 sticks of butter

¾ cup brown sugar

¾ cup white sugar

1 tsp baking soda

½ tsp salt

2 eggs

2 ¼ cup of flour

2 cup of chocolate chips

INSTRUCTIONS

1. Beat together softened butter with all the sugar.
2. Add eggs and beat well.
3. Sprinkle in salt and baking soda.
4. Add the flour and mix well.
5. Add chocolate chips.
6. Rest in the fridge for 10 minutes.
7. Tablespoon size balls onto cookie sheets.
8. Bake at 375 for 9 min.

NOTE: I discovered by mistake one day that if you withhold the eggs you'll make a very crispy and crumbly cookie.

WHITE RASPBERRY COOKIES

INGREDIENTS

1 ¼ cup flour

1 tbsp baking powder

½ tsp salt

1 stick of butter

½ cup brown sugar

¼ cup white sugar

1 box jello cheesecake

3-6 tbsp raspberry jam

INSTRUCTIONS

Follow 1-7 listed above but include Jello cheesecake last. Then flatten dough down, create divots, add in jam then bake at 375 for 12 min.

PEANUT BUTTER COOKIES

INGREDIENTS

1 cup peanut butter

1 tsp baking soda

1 tsp salt

1 egg

1 tsp vanilla extract.

INSTRUCTIONS

Follow 1-7 (leave out the chocolate chips),

For better texture, lightly push the cookie dough balls down, then imprint a fork vertically and horizontally to create a criss-cross pattern.

PANTRY & PRESERVATION

COOKIES (ORANGE, LEMON & SUGAR)

• Freezer Friendly

INGREDIENTS

ORANGE

1 cup white sugar

1 cup butter

½ cup buttermilk

2 eggs

½ baking soda

1 tsp baking powder

½ tsp salt

3 cups flour

1 orange (juice)

FROSTING

2 tbsp butter

1 cup powdered sugar

2 tbsp orange juice

INSTRUCTIONS

1. Mix butter and sugar, eggs first until creamy.
2. Add in all other ingredients and mix well.
3. Place dough onto lined cookie sheet in tablespoon sized balls. Bake at 350 for 10-12 minutes.
4. Cool cookies on drying rack.
5. Mix frosting ingredients and apply on top of cookies.

LEMON COOKIES

INGREDIENTS

2 cups flour

1/2 tsp baking powder

½ tsp baking soda

½ tsp salt

½ cup butter

1 cup sugar

8 oz riccotta cheese (room temp)

Zest 1 lemon

1 egg

2 tsp vanilla extract

1 cup powdered sugar

INSTRUCTIONS

1. Mix butter and gran. sugar, then add in ricotta, zest mix again.
2. Beat in eggs, vanilla extract.
3. Slowly mix in dry ingredients.
4. Place dough balls on cookie sheet.
5. Bake for 10-12 minutes at 350 degrees, cool on rack after.

SOFT SUGAR COOKIES

INGREDIENTS

2 ½ cup flour

2 tsp baking powder

¾ tsp salt

2 sticks butter

1 ¼ cup sugar

1 egg + 1 egg yolk

1 tsp vanilla extract

INSTRUCTIONS

1. Large bowl/mixer mix soft butter, sugar, eggs.
2. Then add in dry ingredients, mix by hand.
3. roll out dough or balls onto cookie sheet.
4. Bake 10-12 minutes at 350, cool on rack after.

PANTRY & PRESERVATION

WHOOPIE PIES

• Freezer Friendly

INGREDIENTS

1 cup butter

2 cups sugar

2 eggs+ 2 egg yolks

1 cup cocoa

2 tsp baking soda

1 tsp baking powder

½ tsp salt

4 cups flour

1 cup buttermilk

1 cup hot water

1 tsp vallia.

FROSTING

See pg _91_

INSTRUCTIONS

1. In a large bowl cream the butter, sugar and eggs.
2. Slowly add in dry ingredients while alternating with liquid ingredients (water/milk).
3. On a lined baking sheet, drop tsp size pieces of the dough.
4. Bake at 350 for 8-10 minutes.
5. Make the frosting by whipping all ingredients together.
6. Allow cookies to cool before applying frosting and covering in a sandwich like style.

MOLASSES COOKIES

INGREDIENTS

¾ cup butter (melted)

1 cup white sugar

1 egg

1/3 cup molasses

2 ¼ cups flour

2 tsp baking soda

1 tsp cinnamon

½ tsp cloves

½ tsp ginger

INSTRUCTIONS

1. In large bowl mix the egg, butter, sugar, and molasses.
2. Then add in all the dry ingredients except the flour.
3. Add the flour by ¼ cup until combined well.
4. Cover/chill dough in the fridge for 30 minutes
5. Bake at 350 for 10-12 min on prelined cookie sheet.

Optional: If desired roll dough bolls in white sugar before baking.

APPLE PIE & PIE CRUST

• Freezer Friendly

INGREDIENTS

FILLING

½ cup butter

3 tbsp flour

3 tbsp water (with/2 tsp cornstarch dissolved in it)

1 tbsp vanilla extract

½ cup white sugar

½ cup brown sugar

2 tsp cinnamon

1 dash" of nutmeg

5 apples of choice (sliced)

EGG WASH

1 egg beaten In 1 tsp of water

Pinch of sugar & cinnamon

INSTRUCTIONS

1. In Medium saucepan melt butter, sprinkle in flour stirring constantly, Cook for 1-2 minutes. Add cornstarch mix, sugar, nutmeg, and cinnamon. Bring to a boil and immediately reduce to simmer/ off heat with lid on for the next 5 minutes.
2. Mix apples into a stovetop dish and allow them to cool off.
3. Roll out ½ of the pie crust, press into pie dish, leaving top off.
4. Pour in apple mix and roll/out cover with the rest of the pie crust.
5. Cut 4 long slices from the center out.
6. Pain on egg wash
7. Cover the pie in tinfoil and bake for 15 min at 425 covered, then for 40 minutes at 350 degrees uncovered.

PIE CRUST

INGREDIENTS

2 ½ cups flour

½ tsp salt

1 cup chilled butter

½ cup cold water

INSTRUCTIONS

1. Add flour and salt into large bowl.
2. Cut cold butter into small cubes and drop into the flour.
3. Using a butter cutter, masher, or a fork mix butter into four until crumbly
4. Add water by tbsp and mix thoroughly until dough-like. I form the ball by hand.
5. Cover dough in saranwrap/ziplock, etc and let rest in fridge for 30-60 min.

APPLE CRISP

• Freezer Friendly

INGREDIENTS

5 cups of peeled/sliced apples

½ tsp cinnamon

1 tsp lemon rind

1 tsp orange rind

1 shot/jigger amaretto liquor

1 shot/jigger Cointreau (orange liquor)

CRUMBLE

¼ cup brown sugar

¾ cup white sugar

¾ cup flour

¼ tsp salt

½ cup cold butter (cubed)

INSTRUCTIONS

1. Grease a casserole dish.
2. peel and slice apples into large bowl.
3. Add cinnamon, lemon rind, orange rind, 1 shot of amaretto liquor, 1 shot of Cointreau (orange liquor).
4. In a medium bowl combine sugar, flour, salt, and cubed cold butter. Mix well.
5. Place apples mixture into casserole then sprinkle the crumble over top.
6. Bake at 350 for 1 hour.

Note: Serve with Ice cream for a real treat.

HOMEMADE ICE CREAM (NO CHURN NEEDED)

INGREDIENTS

VANILLA

1 can of sweetened condensed milk (14 oz)

2 tsp vanilla extract

1/8 tsp salt

2 cups of heavy whipping cream.

CHOCOLATE

Same as above but add

2 tbsp cocoa powder

4 oz of melted semisweet chocolate

INSTRUCTIONS

1. Freeze a metal/glass bowl for at least 15 minutes.
2. In a medium bowl combine the condensed milk, vanilla extract, salt.
3. Remove 1st bowl from the freezer, pour in heavy cream, and beat until fluffy. (about 5-15 minutes depending on if using immersion blender or hand mixer).
4. Pour the 2nd bowl mixture on top of the heavy cream, folding it into the whipped cream.
5. Pour this final bowl into a bread pan and freeze for at least 4 hours.

**When making chocolate ice cream, beat the heavy whipping cream with the cocoa powder, and add the melted chocolate with the condensed milk.

BANANA BREAD

• Freezer Friendly

INGREDIENTS

3-5 smashed bananas (overripe)

2 cups of sifted flour

1 cup granulated sugar

1 stick of butter

2 eggs

1 tsp salt

1 tsp baking soda

1 tsp vanilla extract

INSTRUCTIONS

1. Thaw bananas if frozen previously
2. Add bananas and softened/melted butter into a large bowl. Mix briefly.
3. Add eggs, mix briefly before adding baking soda, salt, and sugar. Mix again.
4. Add in flour by ½ cup at a time. Add in vanilla extract last.
5. Pregrease a bread pan, pour mix in.
6. Bake for 60 min. at 350 degrees. For muffins bake at 325 for 40-60 min or until a toothpick/fork poke is pulled out clean of batter.

ZUCCHINI CINNAMON SWIRL BREAD

INGREDIENTS

1 ½ cup flour

1 1/2 -2 cups grated zucchini

¾ cups sugar

1/3 cup butter

1 tsp vanilla 2 eggs

1 tsp baking soda

½ tsp cinnamon

¼ tsp salt

¼ tsp baking powder

INSTRUCTIONS

1. In a large bowl combine zucchini, sugar, butter, vanilla, eggs.
2. In a smaller bowl combine dry stuff (flour, baking soda & powder, salt, cinnamon) and mix.
3. Add dry ingredients into the first bowl, reuse this bowl for swirling ingredients.
4. Pour 1/3 of batter into pregreased bread pan. Then layer ½ the swirl mix. Then another 1/3 of batter, ½ of swirl, and end with the last 1/3 batter on top.
5. Bake 35-45 min at 350 degrees.

SWIRL

¼ cup brown sugar, 1 tbsp cinnamon

1 tbsp flour.

DONUTS/MAPLE BARS

• (makes 24-donuts)   • Freezer Friendly

INGREDIENTS

½ cup warm water

¾ cup warm milk

2 tsp dry active yeast

½ cup + 1 tbsp gran. Sugar

½ tsp salt

5 large eggs

½ cup butter

5 ½ cup flour

MAPLE DRIZZLE

½ cup maple syrup

¾ cup powdered sugar

3 tbsp softened butter.

(Add tsp of milk if desired for runnier consistency)

INSTRUCTIONS

1. Add water, milk, yeast, 1 tbsp sugar in large bowl. Wait until foamy (5-10 min.)
2. Add flour, salt, eggs, and remaining sugar. If using a mixer, use dough hook attachment and mix ingredients.
3. Add softened butter at high speed until dough is elastic (dough comes off the sides of the bowl)
4. Let rise for 1 hr covered.
5. Punch down dough, rise another hour.
6. punch down, and half the dough into two pieces. Roll out the first half and cut 12 strips, placing onto a cookie sheet for the last rise. Repeat with the other half
7. Let rise another 30 min.
8. Bring frying oil to 330-360 degrees in
9. Drop in dough pieces a few at a time and cook for ~1-2 minutes on each side. Use a slotted spoon to place into and remove donuts.
10. Placed donuts on a plate covered in paper towels.
11. Cover in icing as desired.

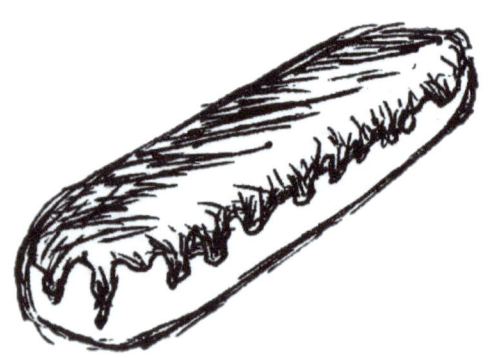

BROWNIES (HEALTHY VS FUDGY)

INGREDIENTS

1 banana, 1 cup grated carrots

1 cup spinach, cup grated zucchini

¼ cup coconut oil

¼ cup milk

1/3 cup honey

1 tsp baking soda

1 tsp baking powder

1 tsp vanilla extract

1/14 cup flour

1/3 cup cocoa powder

¼ tsp salt

¼ cup chocolate chips/chunks

INSTRUCTIONS

1. Blend all wet ingredients (veggies, liquids) in a blender.
2. In a medium bowl mix dry ingredients together and pour in the blender batter. Mix well, add in chocolate chips.
3. Grease casserole dish or muffin pans, pour batter in.
4. Bake for 20 min at 350 degrees.

EASY FUDGY BROWNIES (9X9 PAN)

INGREDIENTS

1 10 tbsp butter

1 ¼ cup sugar

¾ cup cocoa powder

½ tsp salt

1 tsp baking powder

1 tsp vanilla extract

2 large eggs

½ cup flour.

Optional topping of chocolate chips.

INSTRUCTIONS

1. butter your 9x9 dish.
2. mix butter, sugar until fluffly with whisk (about 4 minutes high speed). Then addd in eggs, then cocoa. lightly
3. Add remaining flour, salt, baking powder, vanilla extract lightly mixing together (try not to overmix with these last ingredients)
4. Pour mix into dish & bake for 30-35 min at 325 degrees.

PANTRY & PRESERVATION

CHEESECAKE & SOFT CARAMELS

• Freezer Friendly

INGREDIENTS

3 of the 8 oz cream cheese blocks

¾ cup sugar

3 eggs

1 tsp vanilla extract

CRUST

1 ½ cup graham cracker

 (or chocolate wafers, etc)

¼ cup melted butter.

(See Lemon bar CRUST recipe on PG _62_ as an alternative.)

INSTRUCTIONS

1. Melt butter and smash the crackers you plan on using for the crust. (via a blender/processor, or by hand inside a Ziplock)
2. combine the two and press into a pie pan.
3. Soften the cream cheese, then whip/beat the cream cheese and sugar until fluffy.
4. Add in eggs one at a time, mix well.
5. Pour into pie plan and bake for 35-45 minutes at 350 degrees.
6. Leave to cool then refrigerate for 4+ hours before enjoying!.

SOFT CARAMELS CANDY/DRIZZLE

INGREDIENTS

1 cup powdered sugar

¼ cup water

1 tsp salt

7 tbsp butter

½ cup heavy cream

INSTRUCTIONS

1. In a small saucepan add sugar and water, bring to a boil (220 is the key temp),
2. Once the temp is reached remove from heat and pour in melted butter, heavy cream, and salt. Stir until well combined add back to heat until it reaches 220 again.
3. Line a bread pan with parchment or wax paper, pour candy over top & allow to cool. You can cut into it once its set (about 5 hrs/overnight). Sprinkle salt on top & enjoy.

*To enjoy as a **caramel sauce/dip** skip cooling and use right away.

CHOCOLATE & VANILLA CAKE

• Freezer Friendly

INGREDIENTS

CHOCOLATE

2 eggs

½ cup cocoa

1 cup butter

3 cups flour

1 cup buttermilk

2 tsp vanilla

1 tsp salt

1 tsp baking soda

2 cups sugar

1 cup boiling water.

INSTRUCTIONS

1. Add ingredients in the order listed to the left.
2. Mix once all ingredients except the boiling water, then pour the boiling water over top and mix.
3. Pre greased & floured (sift scant amount of flour overtop) a 9x12 pan.
4. Pour into pan & bake 25-30 min at 350 degrees. Or until a toothpick or fork stab comes out clean.

NOTE: For **Cake pops**, immediately use a mixer with paddle attachement & mix the hot cake. The heat & humidity will make it doughy, you then form into balls, freeze, and dip in melted chocolate before serving.

VANILLA CAKE (2 CAKE ROUND PANS)

INGREDIENTS

2 cups flour

2 ½ tsp baking powder

4 eggs

1 ½ cups granulated sugar

1 cup milk

1 stick butter

3 tsp vanilla extract

3 tsp coconut oil

¼ tsp salt

INSTRUCTIONS

1. Add all eggs into a large bowl and beat/mix on a medium speed for about 1 minute, pour in sugar beating for 1 more minute.
2. Increase to high speed for 8 minutes.
3. In a different bowl combine all dry ingredients, soften/melt coconut oil, butter and mix in vanilla extract. Add milk to this wet mixture.
4. lightly whisk in the flour about ½ cup at a time scattering evenly over the surface before stirring. (don't over stir)
5. Slowly whisk in oil/butter/milk/vanilla mix over the eggs/flour.
6. Pour batter into the cake pan, lightly dropping the pan to remove large bubbles.
7. Bake for 30 minutes at 350 degrees.
8. Allow to cool before layering with frosting. (See pg _91_ for frosting recipe

PANTRY & PRESERVATION 57

CARROT "SPICE" CAKE

• Freezer Friendly

INGREDIENTS

¼ cup melted coconut oil or butter

½ cup white sugar

1 large egg

2 tsp baking powder

½ tsp salt

1 tsp cinnamon

1 ½ cup flour

½ cup milk

2 cups finely shredded carrots.

INSTRUCTIONS

1. Add all ingredients except flour and carrots in a large bowl. Mix well.
2. Add flour, mix, and then carrots and mix.
3. Pour batter into a pregreased 9x9 casserole dish or cake pan.
4. In a small bowl combine streusel ingredients by hand and sprinkle by hand over top the cake.
5. Bake 25-35 min at 350 degrees.

STRUESAL

½ cup brown sugar

2 tbsp flour

2 tsp cinnamon

2 tbsp butter

*Optional: Drizzle with cream cheese icing, see page _91_*

58 PANTRY & PRESERVATION

BLACKBERRY COBBLER CAKE

• Freezer Friendly

INGREDIENTS

2 medium bags of blackberries

2 cups flour

1 cup white sugar

1 orange (for zest)

1-2 tsp lemon juice

1 stick butter

1 ½ cup milk

3 tsp baking powder

1 tsp salt.

TOPPING

¼ cup brown sugar

¼-1/2 stick of butter (melted)

1 cup of oats

1 tbsp cinnamon

INSTRUCTIONS

1. Add sugar, zest, juice, and blackberries into a large bowl. Stir and sit for 20 minutes until syrupy.

2. In a different medium bowl combine dry ingredients, the milk and butter.

3. Grease a 9x13 dish, pour ½ of the #2 batter as the initial layer. Pour in black berries evenly then scatter/plop in remainder of the #2 batter randomly on top.

4. New bowl combine all the topping ingredients and sprinkle on top.

5. Bake for 1 hour at 375 degrees.

(Add another 10 minutes if too doughy)

PANTRY & PRESERVATION

LEMON BLUEBERRY MUFFINS

• Freezer Friendly

INGREDIENTS

MUFFINS

2 cups of flour

¾ cup white sugar

¾ cup milk

2 ½ tsp baking powder

2 eggs (room temp)

½ cup coconut oil

Zest & juice of 1 lemon

1-2 cups of blueberries

STRUESAL TOPPING

1/3 cup flour

3 tbsp butter

3 tbsp dark brown sugar

¼ tsp cinnamon powder

INSTRUCTIONS

1. In a large bowl add all muffin ingredients except the blueberries and mix until well combined. Fold in blueberries lightly coated in flour.

2. Pregrease Muffin pans with butter or use small parchment paper. Pour in muffin batter until it reaches just under the rim.

3. In a smaller bowl combine streusel topping, mix well.

4. Drop the streusel by hand each muffin over top.

5. Bake at 375 for 18-22 minutes or until a fork/toothpick comes out clean

NOTE: For **lemon poppyseed muffins**, add in 1 tbsp of poppyseed into batter, withhold the blueberries & streusel.

LEMON BARS (9X13 CASSEROLE DISH)

INGREDIENTS

½ cup flour

Zest of 3 lemons

1 cup of lemon juice

3 cups sugar

8 eggs

CRUST

2 ½ cup flour

12 tbsp butter (melted)

2/3 cup powdered sugar

½ tsp salt

INSTRUCTIONS

1. Whisk all Crust ingredients until well combined and dough like.

2. Pregrease casserole dish or line with parchment. Pour in the curst dough, wet your finger and push until evenly spread throughout the dish. Bake at 350 for 20 minutes.

3. Using a high speed blender or food processor mixing the sugar and zest (can do by hand too but the bars will be more chunky).

4. Combine sugar/zest in a large bowl with flour, lemon juice, and eggs. Whisk until well combined. For very fine texture us a sifter when adding the flour.

5. Pour over a warm crust & bake in the oven for another 25 minutes (still at 350). Cool in the fridge for about 1-2 hours.

GUMMIES/FRUIT LEATHERS

INGREDIENTS

FRUIT LEATHER

2 cups of fruit/veggie mix.

½ cup of water

1 tbsp honey or maple syrup.

INSTRUCTIONS

1. Soften any hard veggies or fruit by boiling them. Strain and add to high powered blender.
2. Add in sweetner honey/maple syrup. Blend lightly.
3. Add in water by tbsp until thick enough to pour but not runny.
4. Prepare parchemnt paper or silicon mats on a cookie sheet.
5. Preheat oven to lowest temperature and dehydrate until lightly tacky to touch, but solid (approx 4/5 hours). If using a dehydrator, do so for at 135 for about 5 hours..

GUMMIES

INGREDIENTS

2 cups of blended fruit of choice

1 cup of water

(Increase to 1 1/2 cup for thicker fruits like apples/bananas)

2-4 tbsp unflavored gelatin or 2 packets.

(depends on desired hardness)

INSTRUCTIONS

1. Blend desired fruit/veggies nd pour into small saucepan with water. Bring to a boil and immediately remove from heat. Strain through mesh if desired to remove skins/seeds.
2. Sprinkle in gelatin and mix well until fully dissolved.
3. Pour into medium sized casserole dish or into silicone mold shapes and place in fridge for 2-3 hours or until Jello-like. For firmer gummies use an extra tbsp of gelatin.

HINT-I like to add in shredded carrots/ broccoli stems, spinach for added nutrition.

GUSHERS

**For gusher like gummies, fill molds halfway cool, then add a mashed fruit + arrowroot powder puree to center of molds, cool then pour other half of gelatin on top of mold.

YOGURT & DRINKS

INGREDIENTS

2 tbsp plain yogurt

½ gall of whole milk

**Strain through cheese cloth for "Greek yogurt".

Flavor with honey & fruit of choice.

Note: Dehydrate yogurt into powder at 135 degrees for 10 hours in dehydrator.

INSTRUCTIONS

Stovetop. Large pot bring milk to 180, then remove from heat.

Cool until about 100-110.

Remove 1 cup of warm milk, stir in the 2 tbsp of yogurt. Pour this back into the large pot stir well then cover & keep at 90-100 degrees for 8 hours.

Instant pot. Press yogurt button twice, it will boil to 180 automatically. Remove the pot from machine to cool to 110. Remove a cup of warm milk, stir in the 2 tbsp of yogurt, pour back in/ stir well. Remove silicone ring from instant pot lid, place back on & press yogurt button for 8 hours (it will count up in time.)

Store in airtight container in fridge (good for about 1-2 weeks).

YOGURT DRINKS

INGREDIENTS

2-3 cups of fruit

2 tbsp honey

4 cups yogurt

(see Pg __ on how to make yogurt)

INSTRUCTIONS

1. Chop up larger fruit, and place fruit into a food processor or high-speed blender.
2. Add in honey & blend.
3. Pour in Plain Yogurt & pulse for about 5 seconds at most.
4. Store in an airtight container in the fridge for up to 1-2 weeks.

BARS (CHICKPEA & GRANOLA)
• Freezer Friendly

INGREDIENTS

¾ cups rolled oats

1 can chickpeas

(or 14 oz aka garbanzos)

½ cup peanut butter

¼ cup maple syrup

1 tsp vanilla extract

½ tsp cinnamon

½ baking powder

[2 tbsp chickpea water from can or from boiling on stovetop]

TOPPING

¼ cup coconut oil

¼ cup cocoa powder

2-3 tbsp maple syrup

Salt from sprinkling

(optionally add nuts, chia seeds, quinoa etc)

INSTRUCTIONS

1. Using a blender or food processor add in oats and blend until close to flour consistency.
2. Add in chickpeas and blend.
3. Add in maple syrup, peanut butter, vanilla extract, cinnamon, baking powder, blend until it comes off the sides of the food processor/ stiff like dough.

   (Add in more chickpea water as needed if too stiff).
4. Line a cookie sheet with parchment, press the dough until about about ¼ in thick. Should fill a normal rectangular size cookie sheet. (wet fingers to press down)
5. Bake 18-20 min at 350 degrees.
6. Let cool, p*rep the topping by melting coconut oil in a small saucepan. Add maple syrup, then cocoa powder. Whisk until smooth.*
7. Add additional toppings before pouring chocolate topping. Freeze for 30 minutes then enjoy.

SOURDOUGH GRANOLA BARS

INGREDIENTS

½ cup sourdough discard

1 cup flour

2 cups oats

½ cup coconut oil

1/3 cup honey (or maple syrup)

1 tsp salt

1/3 cup jam

INSTRUCTIONS

1. Mix all ingredients (except jam) until well combined.
2. Divide the mixture in half. Preline a 8x8 or 13x4 dish with parchment paper. Press in half of mixture.
3. Layer jam onto of dough leaving ½ inch border around each edge.
4. Drop clumps of dough on top of jam, and lightly smooth out dough to cover all of jam (don't press too hard & lose your jam).
5. Bake at 350 degrees for about 35 minutes.

PANTRY & PRESERVATION

DISCARD CRACKERS/CEREAL

• Freezer Friendly

INGREDIENTS

2 tbsp butter (melted0)

1 cup flour

¾ cup sourdough discard

¾ cup cheddar cheese

(or any cheese available)

Salt for sprinkling.

Optional: Add in/sprinkle mutliple seasonings for variety (ex. Rosemary garlic, everything bagel seasoning, paprika, etc.)

INSTRUCTIONS

1. Combine all ingredients in a medium bowll into a dough like ball. (include desired seasonings now)
2. Roll out dough into a large rectangle (enough to nearly fill a average cookie sheet)
3. Use a pizza cutter/pasta cutter or knife to precut dough into desired cracker size. Sprinkle with salt.
4. Bake at 375 for 10-13 minutes. (or until desired crispiness)
5. Store in airtight container for up to 3 days or freeze to keep fresh.

CEREAL/GRAHAM CRACKERS

INGREDIENTS

1 ½ cups flour

¼ cup sugar

1 tbsp cinnamon

½ cup sourdough discard

1 tsp vanilla extract

TOPPING

¼ cup butter, ½ cup sugar

1 tbsp cinnamon

INSTRUCTIONS

Follow above instructions 1-5.

Feel free to lightly dust with white sugar/cinnamon once cooled.

For swirl design, mix the ingredients in two separate bowls, cut cold butter into the topping mix before combining with the other dough, roll out.

CREAMER, SYRUP, MARSHMALLOWS

COFFEE CREAMER (3 CUPS)

INGREDIENTS

1 cup brown sugar

½ cup water

1 cup heavy cream

¾ cup whole milk

1 tsp vanilla extract

1 tsp pumpkin pie spice

or other Flavoring of choice

(cinnamon, nutmeg, cacao etc. seasoning, use approximately 1 tsp)

INSTRUCTIONS

1. In a medium saucepan add brown sugar, then pour water over top. Turn on heat to medium/high.
2. Stir until sugar is fully dissolved. Then add seasoning such as pumpkin pie spice. Simmer for 5 minutes then remove from heat.
3. Add in vanilla extract, then the heavy cream and milk stirring well.
4. Pour into a container of choice (I prefer to use large mason jars with lids), allow to cool before placing into the fridge with lid.

Good for about 1 week.

CHOCOLATE SYRUP

(~2 cups) | Add 1-2 tsp to 1 cup of milk for chocolate milk.

INGREDIENTS

1 ½ cup water, 1 ½ cup white sugar

1 cup cocoa powder, 1 tsp vanilla extract, 1 pinch salt.

INSTRUCTIONS

1. In small saucepan combine water, sugar, cocoa powder, salt and whisk constantly over med-high heat (must reach 220 degrees to thicken correctly).
2. Remove from heat, stir in extract. Store in airtight container in the fridge.

MARSHMALLOWS

For "mini" marshmellows you can add mix to ziplock & pipe out logs.h & allow to harden in log shape. Cut with scissors for the traditional shape.

INGREDIENTS

1 cup water

¼ cup gelatin (4 tbsp)

1 cup of honey/syrup/sugar

1 tbsp marshmallow root

1/8 cup powdered sugar

Starch for dusting (for an easier cutting/serving dust the top of finished mix with starch of choice)

INSTRUCTIONS

1. In a small bowl stir marshmallow root into a warm cup of water, Set aside for 10 min.
2. Strain liquid. Divide in half, ½ cup in a bowl whisk with gelatin, the other half into a saucepan with the sweetener. Bring to a boil (Reach 220-240 degrees)
3. Beat the gelatin on high, pour hot mix over top. Beat for 4 min or until fluffy, then pour into 9x13 prebuttered dish. Cool in fridge 4 hrs. Store in airtight container on the counter.

BREADS

GYRO/PITA BREAD
• Freezer Friendly

INGREDIENTS

4 cups of flour

¾ cups warm water

1 package dry yest (2 ¼ tsp)

1 tsp + 1 tbsp sugar

1 ½ tsp salt

3 tbsp olive oil

¾ cup cup plain greek yogurt

(or strain whole plain yogurt).

(ALTERNATIVELY, You can cook the pitas: 2-4 min each side cooking in a skillet at med/high heat, one by one).

INSTRUCTIONS

1. Warm the water, then combine with the yeast and sugar in a large bowl. Wait until frothy (~5 min)
2. Then add in flour, salt, sugar, oil, yogurt and mix.
3. Knead dough for about 7-10 minutes or until slightly sticky (add flour as needed).
4. Place dough into a oiled bowl and cover to rise for about 1-2 hours.

   (TIP: place someplace warm to decrease the rise time)
5. Dust a counterspace with flour, dump dough on top and divide into 12 balls. Place onto a cookie sheet/cover and rise another 20 minutes.
6. Roll out each dough ball by hand, use your finger to naturally make dimples into the dough to a ¼ inch thickness.
7. Space out onto 2 different cookie sheets and bake in oven at 500 for 5-8

TORTILLA (16 TORTIILLAS)

INGREDIENTS

3 cups of flour

1 tsp salt

1 tsp baking powder

1/3 cup of oil (olive/avocado)

1 cup **warm water**.(not cold/not hot)

INSTRUCTIONS

1. Combine all dry ingredients in a large bowl. Then pour in oil/water to its center. Stir until dough can form into a ball.
2. Dump onto floured surface and knead until smooth. (Can just use a dough hook on a mixer for about 2-3 minutes).
3. Divide dough into 18 pieces. And roll each piece into about 6 inches wide circles.
4. Heat a skillet to med/high, cook tortillas for about 1 minutes, flip and cook ½ min. (Lightly browned is the goal).
5. Stack/cover finished tortillas to keep warm/soft. Eat now or keep in the fridge for 5 days, or freeze in an airtight container.

CHEESY DROP BISCUITS

• Freezer Friendly

INGREDIENTS

1 ½ cup flour

2 tsp baking powder

1 tsp salt

4 oz butter (cold/cubed)

¾ cups of milk

1 cup cheese (of choice)

INSTRUCTIONS

1. Mix flour, baking powder, salt until crumbly. (cut in butter with butter cutter, fork or use a food processor until crumbly)
2. Add in cheese, mix.
3. Add in milk and mix.
4. Drop dough blobs onto a prelined baking sheet. (about a 2 tbsp).
5. Bake for 15-20 min at 400 degrees.

BUTTERMILK BISCUITS

INGREDIENTS

2 ½ cups flour

2 tbsp baking powder

1 tsp salt

2 tsp honey

½ cup butter (cold/cubed)

1 cup+2 tbsp cold buttermilk

INSTRUCTIONS

1. Mix all dry ingredients, then cut in the cold butter until crumbly.
2. Add in cold buttermilk, honey, combine until doughlike.
3. Roll out dough then fold into itself. Left to center, right side to center. Rotate, and roll out again.

    Fold inwards again (repeat 2 x).
4. Roll out until about 1 inch thick.
5. Cut out using cookie cutter (don't twist), and place onto a pregreased cast iron skillet (8-10 biscuits) Bake for 15-18 minutes at 425.

HAWAIIAN/DINNER ROLLS

• (24 rolls)   • Freezer Friendly

INGREDIENTS

1 ½ cup pineapple juice

4 ½ tsp active yeast

2/3 cup white sugar

½ cup butter (softened)

1 tsp vanilla extract

2 eggs

5-6 cups of flour

1 tsp of salt.

INSTRUCTIONS

1. Heat pineapple juice in small saucepan until juice is about 100-110 degrees. Pour into large bowl.
2. Add yeast, sugar allow to froth (~ 5 min)
3. Pour in butter, eggs, and vanilla extract.
4. Using a dough hook, add in flour about ½ cup at a time until dough feels lightly sticky.
5. Cover & rise about 1 hour.
6. Dump onto floured surface and divide dough into 24 rolls. Grease 2 9x13 dishes and place in the dough balls.
7. Cover/rise about 1 hour.
8. Bake at 350 for 20 minutes.

(after removing form oven, brush butter on top for the glossy finish)

PANTRY & PRESERVATION

SANDWICH BREAD

• (2 loaves) • Freezer Friendly

INGREDIENTS

- 2 ¼ cups warm water
- 2 packets dry yeast
- ¼ cup white sugar
- 1 tbsp salt
- ¼ cup oil (or butter)
- 6 ¼ cups all purpose flour

Sourdough alternative

Adjust above recipe to use 2 cups water, 6 cups of flour & ½ cup of active sourdough starter, allow to rise for 4-6 hours, punch down, "walk the dough" until there is surface tension. Dump seam side down into pregreased bread pans & allow to rise another hr. Bake the same.

INSTRUCTIONS

1. 1Warm water, then pour into large bowl, add in yeast and sugar. Allow to froth (~ 5-10 minutes).
2. Add in salt and oil (or butter) Mix in flour 1 cup at a time and use a dough hook if possible. Once lightly sticky (and pulling from the sides) move to preoiled bowl, cover, and rise for 1 hour.
3. Dump dough onto floured surface, divide in half and shape the dough into small logs that will fit in a bread pan.
4. Preoil bread pans and place in dough. Cover, rise for 1 hour.
5. Bake on the lowest rack for 30-35 minutes at 375 (until golden).

Note: Allow bread to cool before cutting into for best texture.

Store in beeswax bags for longest shelf life about 1 week. Freeze to keep fresh.

SOURDOUGH BREAD (ARTISAN)

• Freezer Friendly

INGREDIENTS

3 ½ cup flour

½ cup starter

1 1/3 cup water

2 tsp salt.

Optional: When shaping the dough (step_5_) add in extra seasoning(rosemary, garlic, etc) or even whole ingredients (garlic, cubed cheese, etc.) Sprinkle on the rectangle and initial fold.

NOTE: (I personally leave the dough somewhere warm all day, and come do these pull/fold when I think about it. I am not strict with the time or amount).

INSTRUCTIONS

1. Combine warm water, and starter, mix well.

2. Add in salt and flour, knead until combined. Transfer to oiled bowl. Cover/rest for 30 minutes then grab the edge of dough, pull up and over x4. Cover & rest another 30 minutes. Repeat one more time.

3. Once the dough appears to have doubled in size. Dump onto floured surface for shaping.

4. Pull dough into a rectangle shape. Pull right and left sides of the rectangle into the center where they will meet. Then roll the dough towards yourself to cover the seam.

5. Place the bread seam down and lightly move the bread at the bottom only to gather tension on the dough (see pic)

6. In a floured bowl or place a dish towel covered in flour into a bowl, place the dough seam side up. Cover and allow to ferment in the fridge overnight (or at least 3 hours).

7. Place dutch oven or lided bread pan into oven, preheat to 500.

8. Remove dough from fridge, dump onto parchment paper. Cut at least one long/deep slit into the bread to allow steam out. (feel free to be decorative).

9. Put dough into preheated dutch oven for 20 min, then 8 min uncovered at 500.

SOURDOUGH BAGUETTES

• Freezer Friendly

INGREDIENTS

1 ¼ cup warm water

2 cups sourdough starter

4 ½-5 cups flour

2 ½ tsp salt

2 tsp sugar

1-2 tsp instant yeast

4 tsp chia seeds

INSTRUCTIONS

1. Warm water, and mix with starter & yeast. Mix in 3 cups of flour.
2. Add in chia seeds, salt, and another 1 ½ to 2 cups of flour.
3. Knead for about 7 minutes. Then place into preoiled bowl.
4. Cover/rise about 90 minutes.
5. Dump dough onto floured surface, and divide into 3 loafs, roll out into rope like shape.
6. Using tinfoil under parchment paper create two lengthwise wall shapes on a cookie sheet. Place each section of dough onto the sheet (so that the dough is supported to keep its shape-see picture)
7. Cover and let rise another 1 1/2-2 hrs.
8. Slash 3 cuts into each bagguette for flatter bread or leave alone.
9. Bake for 25 minutes at 450. (toss in a few cubes of ice at the bottom for crispier outside)
10. Remove the bread from cookie sheet and place back into the oven right on the rack for another 5-10 minutes after turning the oven off for crunchier bread.

SOURDOUGH BAGELS

• Freezer Friendly

INGREDIENTS

½ cup sourdough starter

1 cup 1 tbsp warm water

2 tbsp honey

2 tsp salt

4 cups + 2 tbsp flour

INSTRUCTIONS

1. Warm water, then add to large bowl. Add in starter, honey and salt and mix well.

2. Add in flour and mix well. Knead for 6-10 minutes to create a nice and firm dough.

3. Transfer to preoiled bowl, cover, rise for 8-12 hours.

4. Dump dough onto floured surface and divide into 12-16 balls. Now either push through the center to make a hole and stretch out the dough into bagel shape OR

    Log roll the dough, attach the edges by stretching one edge over the other, pinching edges together nicely. Place bagels onto two cookie sheets spaced well.

5. Cover/rise another 30-60 minutes.

6. Preheat oven to 425, while bringing a large pot of water to a boil (at least 2 inches deep with water.)

7. Add in a tbsp of baking soda, and of brown sugar to the large pot.

8. Drop in bagels to pot a few at a time, cooking for 1-2 minutes, flipping and cooking another 1 minute. After removing bagel from water, dust with salt or other preferred seasoning. Repeat until all bagels have been boiled.

9. Bake bagels for 20-25 minutes at 425 or until golden brown.

PIZZA DOUGH/SOUR-PIZZA-DO

• Freezer Friendly

INGREDIENTS

1 cup warm water

1 tbsp sugar

1 tbsp yeast

1 tbsp oil

2-2 ½ cups flour

1 tsp salt

INSTRUCTIONS

1. Warm water, pour into large bowl. Add in yeast, and sugar. Wait until frothy (~5 minutes).

2. Stir in olive oil, then flour. Combine until doughlike. Dump onto floured surface and knead until a ball forms. Place back into oiled bowl, cover and rest 10 min-1 hour.

3. Roll out dough into typical shape of pizza, add your toppings/sauce and bake 12-15 minutes at 500 degrees

LARGE SOURDOUGH FLAT PIZZA

INGREDIENTS

1 cup sourdough starter

½-3/4 cup warm water

2 ½ cup flour

1 tsp salt

(For thicker rising, cover dough to rise for 30min-1 hr after rolling out).

INSTRUCTIONS

1. Mix all ingredients in medium sized bowl. Knead until a dough ball, Transfer to oiled bowl.

2. Cover/rise 2-4 hours.

3. Dump out and create 2 medium or 1 large sheet pan pizza dough, roll out dough. Brush with oilive oil and let rest for 15 minutes.

4. Add toppings/sauce as desired and cook 10 minutes at 450. Top with fresh cheese and cook another 5-7 minutes.

GLUTON FREE FAVORITES

• (Artisan Loaf & Cinnamon Rolls)   • Freezer Friendly

INGREDIENTS

3 ¾ cups gluten free flour

1 packet dry yeast

1 tbsp xantham gum (1 tbsp)

2 cups of warm water

1 tbsp sugar

2 tsp baking powder

2 tsp apple cider vinegar

2 eggs

INSTRUCTIONS

1. In a bowl combine the yeast, sugar, & warm water. Rest until frothy (5 min)
2. In a large bowl combine all dry ingredients, eggs, vinegar, and Step 1 bowl. Use a dough hook, or knead by hand until dough like ball(~5 min). Cover/rise 1 hr.
3. Insert an empty dutch oven into the oven & preheat to 450.
4. Dump onto floured parchment, slice 2-3 cuts. Pull out dutch oven, put in the bread & bake for 45 minutes covered, 5 minutes uncovered.
5. Allow to cool, then slice & enjoy.

CINNAMON ROLLS

INGREDIENTS

3 ¼ cup gluten free flour (With xantham gum)

1 cup warm milk (110 degrees)

1 tbsp of instant yeast

¼ cup butter

2 eggs

1 tsp apple cider vinegar

½ cup white sugar

3 tsp baking powder

½ cup heavy whipping cream.

Pinch of salt

FILLING

¼ cup butter, 1 cup brown sugar, 1 tbsp flour, 1 ½ tbsp cinnamon

INSTRUCTIONS

1. Start by mixing the warm milk with sugar and the yeast. Allow to foam about 5 minutes.
2. Mix in the eggs and apple cider vinegar.
3. Add in the gluten free flour, baking powder and salt into the bowl, then the melted butter until fully combined.
4. Use a dough hook or dust a counter and knead for about 5-10 minutes (or until the dough comes off the sides of the bowl). It is a stickier dough, don't add extra flour.
5. Place dough ball into a pre-oiled bowl. Cover & rise about 20 minutes.
6. Mix all filling ingredients in a small bowl & dust a clean counter or parchment paper.
7. Dump dough onto area, and roll out to a large rectangle (about ½ inch thick). Spread cinnamon mix on top, patting into the dough.
8. Cut strips into the dough About 1 inch wide. And roll them towards you. Pour a small amount of heavy cream into the bottom of casserole dish, and place cinnamon rolls in.
9. Warm the heavy cream and pour overtop the rolls.
10. Bake rolls at 375 for 15-20 minutes. Cool, then frost with icing of choice.

FRIDGE & PANTRY FROM SCRATCH

SOURDOUGH STARTER

INGREDIENTS

300 g all purpose flour

400 g whole grain flour

800 g water (filtered)

1 cup~225 g

1 tbsp~15 g

NOTE: Once established follow a 1:1:1 ratio. So if you are feeding your starter. Whatever amount you had left in your jar, you can pour in that equal amount of water and flour. (ex. ¼ cup starter, ¼ cup flour, ¼ cup water).

I don't follow grams for many of my recipes, I don't always remember to feed my starter. That's okay, it has protective mechanisms (hooch for example is a protective barrier).

Creating the starter can seem daunting but once established it is a very low maintenance item. If you can get starter from a friend with an established starter I'd recommend it, but in case you don't, this recipe is here to use!

Most baking recipes you can replace a dry yeast with sourdough starter just remove about 2 tablespoons of flour & 2 tbsp of liquid from the recipe & replace it with 4 tbsp of sourdough starter. Increase rise times by about 3-6 hours as well.

INSTRUCTIONS

Day 1: Clean jar thoroughly. Add 100 g whole rye flour w/125 g warm water. Keep out on the counter/covered with breathable fabric (or coffee filter) for 24 hours.

Day 2: Pour 75 g of that mixture into a new clean jar (discard the rest).

Add 50 g whole flour, 50 g all purpose, 115 g warm water. Mix well with clean spoon. Keep out/covered for 24 hours

Day 3: Repeat day 2 steps.

Day 4: Repeat day 2 steps in the morning and in the evening (twice in one day)

Day 5: Repeat day 4 steps (feed twice a day)

Day 6: Same as day 5

Day 7: Pour only 20 g into new clean jar, 30 g whole rye, 70g all purpose flour, 100 g water.

Now it should be established enough to use in sourdough recipes!.

(Keep in the fridge between using, Hooch will form on top of the starter over time. It is a protective barrier of alcohol & water, this is normal! Pour that out and continue as usual.)

KOMBUCHA

• (1/2 gallon-4 bottles)   • Freezer Friendly

INGREDIENTS

6 cups of water(filtered)

4 tea bags (black or green tea)

½ cup sugar

1 cup starter scoby.

LITMUS PAPER(Acidity tester easily ordered on Amazon)

Proper acidity prevents botulism.

NOTE: If you overfermented your kombucha and its too acidic that is okay! Use it like you would apple cider vinegar.

I use it in my chickens water feeder, and in cooking recipes.

INSTRUCTIONS

1. Boil water in large pot. Steep the tea for about 20 minutes. Remove from heat, stir in sugar until dissolved. Pour into a half gallon jar if you have one, place breathable material on top.

2. Allow to cool to room temperature.

3. Add in the scoby & cup of starter juice.

4. Cover/ferment 5-7 days. Place in a dark place for faster results. The goal is to get a thin scoby to form on top of the liquid and to reach a ph 2.5-3.5. Take a spoonful of liquid out to test with litmus paper.

5. Once ready reserve 1 cup of the solution with the scoby chunk in a mason jar and store for future uses.

6. Presterilize your bottles via boiling water, then add in your flavoring. I always add about a tbsp of freshly diced ginger, then other flavors like a tbsp or 2 of blackberries, pineapples, lime, etc.

7. Pour original solution into bottles up to the neck curve of the bottle (about a cup ½) Cap the bottles and allow to ferment 5-7 days.

NOTE: Glass can explode from pressure, check your bottles to see of they are fizzy by the 4-5th day. Do this by lightly shaking the bottle, if fiz is seen the drink is ready.

Refrigerate after opening and/or after the 7th day to prevent overfermentation.

SCOBY RECIPE

INGREDIENTS

250 g of tea

2 tbsp sugar

INSTRUCTIONS

Cover with breathable cloth and leave at room temp for about 1 month. Thin white top is the scoby.

APPLE CIDER VINEGAR/ WHITE VINEGAR

INGREDIENTS

1 tbsp sugar: 1 cup filtered water

OR

1 cup sugar: 1 gallon filtered water.

+

Apple scraps prerinsed

*Vinegar can be made from other fruit scraps as well (pear, grapes, plums, oranges, etc).

INSTRUCTIONS

1. Fill a clean jar halfway with fruit scraps.
2. Measure the water as you add it to the jar (enough to cover the scraps).
3. Based on the amount of water you added, Add the sugar. (1 tbsp per cup of water)
4. Stir mixture in jar & cover with breathable material.
5. Store in a dark/warm place, stir at least once a day for 2 weeks.
6. After two weeks, strain out fruit scraps. And cover/ferment the liquid for another 2-3 months.

NOTE: You'll Know it worked when you can smell the vinegar, see the scoby (thin layer at the top of liquid), see the mother (settles at the bottom) or you use the litmus test to show a PH of 3 or under.

OTHER VINEGAR

INGREDIENTS

1 can of beer (ale, lager, stout)

INSTRUCTIONS

Sterilize a wide mouth jar. Pour in beer, cover with breathable material, and set aside/in a dark warm place. Check after 1 month up to 6 months to see if the fermenting has worked.

Look for a thin white barrier on top of the liquid to form. It should also smell like vinegar.

Use a litmus paper to see if PH is at desired acidity. 3, 4 or under.

Once at a level desired transfer to a clean bottle and an airtight seal. Keep in fridge to stop fermentation.

PANTRY & PRESERVATION

FARM CHEDDAR CHEESE

INGREDIENTS

2-2 ½ gallon fresh milk

1/3 cup plain yogurt

(or active kefir 1/8-1/4 cup)

RENNET

2-3 tbsp salt

½-3/4 cup filtered (unchlorinated water)

3-5 tbsp butter/lard.

Apple Cider Vinegar as needed (to wipe away mold over time, then you relather/cover with butter/lard)

NOTE: To remove chlorine from tap water, boil water & let it cool

Or

let tap water sit out overnight, the chllorine will evaporate.

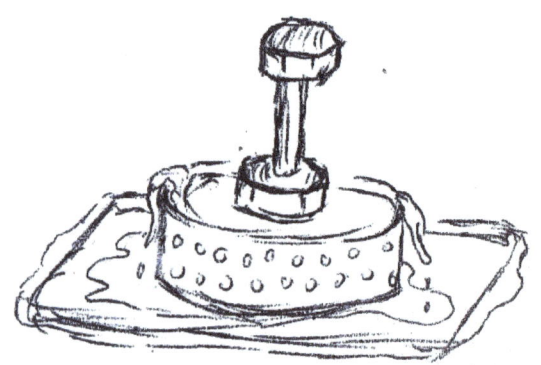

INSTRUCTIONS

1. Pour milk in a medium pot, on medium stirring until 90 degrees F.

2. remove ½ cup of milk, dilute yogurt in it, then whisk back into pot. Stir immediately for 1 minute. Cover/rest 10 minutes.

3. Add rennet (if solid, dilute in water).

4. Using double broiling, place medium pot into a large pot of water, keep the milk at 90-100 degrees.

5. Stir well/quickly for 1 minute then cover/rest for 20-40 minutes or until when you cut into the curd it cuts clean.

6. Cut curds into 1 inch cubes. Stir curds until rounded (~ 15-20 minutes).

   --Prep mold on top of baking sheet to catch any leaking whey__

7. Using a cheesecloth over a cheese press/mold scoop curds into the mold. Once first ½ inch layer is in liberally salt the layer, press firmly down.

8. Continue to add curds to form another layer, liberally salt. Continue a 3rd layer if there are more curds left. Salt then fold the cheese cloth over top.

9. Place lid of mold on the cheese, and add weigh so that there is drips of whey coming out. Let it press this way for 12 hours. Then flip, apply more weight as needed, weigh another 12 hours.

10. Place cheese on a clean plate/cover with a cloth and leave out to harden off.

11. After 3-5 days (or until harderend off) Cover in butter/lard and put away in a fridge or cold place for 3-4 weeks to age. (flip daily).

SOFT CHEESES
• (Mozzeralla, Ricotta, cottage, cream)

MOZZERELLA

INGREDIENTS

5 litres of whole milk

150 ml (.634 cup) of yogurt

3 ml rennet

(if you have no rennet just use 1 tbsp vinegar)

*NOTE: Herbs like nettle, thistle,& yarrow can be distilled to be used as a **rennet**.*

INSTRUCTIONS

1. In a large pot, heat milk on low until it reaches 100 degrees. Then remove from heat. Pull out a cup of milk, mix with the yogurt then add back into large pot.

2. Mix well, then add rennet (or vinegar) Stir gently then cover/rest milk for 15-20 minutes. Curds should form, cut into the thickness horizontally/vertically and stir. Put milk pot into a larger pot of water, to double broil and keep the heat of the milk around 104 degrees. Cover/rest for about 2 hours.

3. Using a cheese cloth over a strainer, strain milk/curds. Don't press out the whey. Keep the warm whey to the side. Try to work the curds from the cheese cloth into a ball shape. Feel free to dip back into the whey to "melt" the mozzeralla. Fold and stretch with a spoon if too hot. Shape into 3 balls and put in a tub of cold water to chill in the fridge (good for 1 week).

RICOTTA/COTTAGE CHEESE

INGREDIENTS

½ gallon whole milk

1/3 cup lemon juice (or vinegar)

1 tsp salt

INSTRUCTIONS

1. Warm milk to 200, add lemon juice/salt and stir.
2. Let sit for 10 min then scoop out any curds that form.
3. Strain through a cheesecloth over 10-60 minutes.

[FOR COTTAGE: leave in more whey/add it back in and leave curd chunks in larger size]

CREAM CHEESE

INGREDIENTS

SAME as ricotta (above)

INSTRUCTIONS

Follow steps 1-2, then squeeze out whey while curds are in cheesecloth. Rinse with cold water, place into a food processor and blend until smooth.

SAUCES
• (Alfredo, Pizza, Pasta, Tomatoe)

ALFREDO

INGREDIENTS

½ cup butter

1 package cream cheese

2 tsp garlic powder

2 cups milk

6 oz parmesan cheese

¼ tsp pepper, 1 tsp salt.

INSTRUCTIONS

1. In a small saucepan melt butter, then cream cheese and seasoning. Whisk until smooth, then slowly pour in milk while whisking.
2. Once smooth again, add in parmesan cheese.
3. Simmer until desired thickness, approx. 5 min.

NOTE: if too thick thin with more milk

PIZZA

INGREDIENTS

6 oz tomato paste

15 oz tomato sauce

1-2 tbsp oregano

2 tbsp italian seasoning

2 tsp garlic

½ tsp onion

1 tsp salt, ½ tsp pepper.

½ tsp sugar

INSTRUCTIONS

Combine paste and sauce until smooth. Pour all seasonings into sauce. Heat to a low-medium heat and simmer for a min of 3 minutes for better flavor.

PASTA

INGREDIENTS

1 can of tomato sauce

2-3 tbsp of Italian seasoning.

½ tsp salt

½ tsp pepper

INSTRUCTIONS

Simmer can of tomato sauce, adding seasoning and simmer for about 5 minutes before pouring over your dinner.

TOMATO SAUCE

INGREDIENTS

4-5 tomatoes

½ cup chopped onion

1 carrot

1 celery stalk

3 cloves of garlic

1 tbsp of olive oil

½ tsp pepper, 1 tsp salt

½ tsp basil

1 tsp honey

3 tbsp lemon juice

INSTRUCTIONS

Heat oil in medium pan, sauté onion, carrots, celery then add in seasoning.

Pour in diced tomatoes, basil and bring to a boil then decrease to a simmer for 20 minutes.

Remove bay leaf.

Blend all ingredients in a blender/food processor. (if you have a food mill you can use it to remove seeds/skins)

Mix in honey and salt/pepper as desired.

**For waterbath canning of pizza/pasta/tomato sauce, place jars with lids in boiling water for 35-40 minutes (for pints or smaller jars).

**ALFEDO sauce requires a pressure canner (10 min at 10 psi for sea level)

OTHER SAUCES

TERRIYAKI

INGREDIENTS

½ cup low sodium soy sauce

½ cup white sugar

¼ cup apple cider vinegar

1 ½ tsp garlic powder

1 tsp onion powder

½ tsp ginger

1 tbsp starch (potato/corn/etc)

INSTRUCTIONS

In a small saucepan combine all ingredients except for the starch. Stir well and then whisk in the cornstarch, bring to a light boil and for about 2-4 minutes stirring constantly. Reduce heat to a simmer. Simmer for 10 minutes, while stirring.

TZATZIKI

INGREDIENTS

1 tbsp olive oil

½ cup grated cucumber

1-2 tbsp lemon juice

1 clove of garlic

½ tsp salt

1 tbsp dill

1 cup whole plain Greek yogurt.

INSTRUCTIONS

In a medium bowl combine all the ingredients. To prevent a runny dip, try squeezing out the cucumber after it had been shredded.

SOY SAUCE

(This takes 6 months to come to fruition)

INGREDIENTS

8 oz of soy beans

12 tbsp

8 tsp salt

½ gallon of filtered water

INSTRUCTIONS

1. Boil soybeans if not precooked/canned soy beans. Simmer for 1-1 1/2 hours until tender. (can use a pressure cooker for 20 minutes). Strain and blend beans.

2. Dump onto floured surface, roll into a log about ¼ inch thick, and cut into ¼ inch slices.

3. Cover in cling wrap/cover with dark cloth and set out for 7 days.

4. Unwrap circles and allow to dry on a large plate/cookie sheet. Once they are brown and dry (koji) they are ready.

5. Using a ½ gallon glass bottle, pour in the water, salt, and Kojji(soy bean disks). Cover, and set aside for 6 months or until koji is dissolved.

6. Strain after through cheese cloth and store in the fridge in a airtight container.

CONDIMENTS

KETCHUP

INGREDIENTS

2 tsp olive oil, 1 chopped onion, 1 clove garlic, 28 oz pureed tomatoes, 1/3 cup dark brown sugar, ¼ cup Apple cider vinegar, 1 tbsp tomato paste, ½ tsp salt, ½ tsp ground mustard, 1/8 tsp ground cloves, 1/8 tsp allspice, 1/8 tsp cayenne.

INSTRUCTIONS

Heat oil/onion until soft. Add in the garlic, tomatoes puree, brown sugar, vinegar, paste, salt, and other seasonings. Bring to a boil then simmer for 45-50 minutes until thickened. Stir occasionally. Once thickened, blend until smooth, and run through a mesh strainer. Store in airtight container in your fridge for up to 3 weeks.

BBQ

INGREDIENTS

1 ½ cup brown sugar, 1 ½ cup ketchup, ½ cup apple cider vinegar, 1 tbsp Worcestershire sauce, 2 tsp paprika, 2 tsp onion powder, 2 tsp salt, 1 tsp pepper

INSTRUCTIONS

In a small saucepan combine all ingredients, bring to a boil, reduce to a simmer for about 15 minutes. Stir consistently throughout.

Store in an airtight container in fridge for about 3 weeks.

MAYO

INGREDIENTS

1 egg, 1 tsp dijon mustard, 1 tsp vinegar, 1 tsp lemon juice, 1 clove garlic minced, 1 cup oil (avocado or veggie-I avoid olive oil), pinch of salt

INSTRUCTIONS

Use high powered blender or immersion blender. In a tall container add the egg, juice, mustard, then garlic. Place immersion blender into container, Lastly pour in the oil letting it clearly separate from bottom ingredients. Mix on high speed until it starts to whiten and slowly raise the blender upward to emulsify the remaining mix.

MUSTARD

INGREDIENTS

¾ cup yellow mustard powder, ¾ tsp salt, ½ tsp turmeric, ¼ tsp garlic powder, 1/8 tsp paprika, ½ cup white vinegar, 1 cup water.

INSTRUCTIONS

In a small saucepan add in all your ingredients except the vinegar. Heat mixture to medium heat, until its simmered down (~30 min) to a paste. Add in the vinegar, mix well, and cook down again to desired thickness. Store in airtight contianer for up to 3 months.

SOUR CREAM

INGREDIENTS

1 cup heavy cream, 2 tsp lemon juice ¼ cup milk

INSTRUCTIONS

Mix in a mason jar, cover with a cover filter/cloth and leave out overnight.

HOMEMADE SEASONING
• (Italian, Taco, Bouillon, Spaghetti)

ITALIAN

INGREDIENTS

2 tsp oregano

1 tsp marjoram

1 tsp thyme

½ tsp basil

½ tsp rosemary & ½ tsp sage

INSTRUCTIONS

Whisk dried ingredients together in small bowl, then store in airtight container. Fresh for at least 6 months.

TACO
(1 lb meat+3/4 cup water+2 tbsp)

INGREDIENTS

2 tbsp chili powder

1 tbsp cumin

2 tsp paprika

1 tsp garlic powder

1 tsp onion powder

1 tsp oregano

1 pinch red pepper flakes

2 tsp salt

1 tsp black pepper.

INSTRUCTIONS

If you want to break it down to make all your seasonings from scratch such as garlic/onion/chives/etc , try finding the herb or ingredient at the market (or grow it yourself in a garden/window). You can dehydrate most items at the lowest setting in your oven for 3-4 hours or once it crumbles at your touch. Then use a coffee grinder to turn into powder and store in an airtight container.

BUILLION
(1 tbsp to 1 cup water)

INGREDIENTS

2 cups nutritional yeast

1/3 cup salt

¼ cup garlic powder

¼ cup onion powder

¼ cup basil

¼ cup oregano & ¼ cup rosemary

2 tbsp black pepper.

INSTRUCTIONS

If you want to break it down to make all your seasonings from scratch such as garlic/onion/chives/etc , try finding the herb or ingredient at the market (or grow it yourself in a garden/window). You can dehydrate most items at the lowest setting in your oven for 3-4 hours or once it crumbles at your touch. Then use a coffee grinder to turn into powder and store in an airtight container.

RANCH
(1 serving: 1 cup mayo: 1 cup buttermilk)

INGREDIENTS

1 tsp parsely

1 tsp salt, ¾ tsp pepper

½ tsp garlic powder

¼ tsp onion powder

1/8 tsp thyme

½ tsp dill

INSTRUCTIONS

If you want to break it down to make all your seasonings from scratch such as garlic/onion/chives/etc , try finding the herb or ingredient at the market (or grow it yourself in a garden/window). You can dehydrate most items at the lowest setting in your oven for 3-4 hours or once it crumbles at your touch. Then use a coffee grinder to turn into powder and store in an airtight container.

PANTRY & PRESERVATION

HOMEMADE EXTRACT & RENNET

VANILLA

INGREDIENTS

8 vanilla beans

1 cup of 80 proof vodka, rum, or brandy.

Bottle with airtight seal.

INSTRUCTIONS

First slice down the middle of each bean, then add to your bottle/jar, pouring the alcohol last. Seal and store in a dark cabinet. Shake at least once a week for the first month, then once every few weeks. (useable within 6 months, but the longer the better!) Label and date, store in cabinet.

MAPLE

INGREDIENTS

½ cup maple syrup

½ cup vodka

INSTRUCTIONS

Pour vodka into container, then maple syrup, stirring very well. Seal with lid, store in a dark cabinet. Shake once a day for a week, then at least once a week after. By week 4 strain mixture into new long term storage container. Label and date, store in cabinet.

LEMON

INGREDIENTS

1 lemon zested

1 cup vodka (80 proof)

Bottle/jar with airtight lid.

INSTRUCTIONS

Wash, dry lemons, then using a peeler or zester cut off the yellow skin (avoid the bitter/white inside). Place peelings into a clean jar ¾ filled, then pour vodka overtop. Seal with lid and shake well. Store in dark cabinet, shake every day for 1 week, then once a week until 6 weeks or longer. (depending on potency you want, you can strain at 6 weeks and store in cabinet, or strain later) Label and date, store in cabinet.

MINT

INGREDIENTS

3 cups mint chopped

1 cup vodka (80 proof)

INSTRUCTIONS

Chop up one cup of the mint, place in jar and cover in alcohol. Store in dark pantry for 1-2 days.

Strain out the mint leaves, then add another fresh cup of chopped leaves. Seal/store. Repeat again with the last cup of mint leaves. Leave this batch for 1-2 weeks in dark cabinet. Strain when you've decided you like the potency of the mint! Label and date, store in cabinet.

RENNET

INGREDIENTS

4-5 cups of water

2 lbs fresh nettle (not gone to seed)..

Ratio 1 cup rennet to 1 gallon milk for cheese.

INSTRUCTIONS

Rinse your herbs free of dirt. Add 2 lbs fresh herb to 4 cups of water in a large pot (or until leaves are covered). Bring to a boil, then reduce to simmer/cover for 30 minutes. Add in 1 tsp salt. Line a strainer with cheesecloth, & place over another bowl. Strain, then store in fridge for up to 2 weeks.

MAPLE SYRUP & EGGNOG

EGGNOG

INGREDIENTS

4 eggs, 1 1/2 cups milk

¾ cup white sugar

½ tsp vanilla extract

½ tsp ground nutmeg

½ cinnamon

1 cups heavy whipping cream

INSTRUCTIONS

1. Beat your eggs in food proccesor/high speed blender for 1 minute.
2. Beat in the sugar, vanilla extract and nutmeg.
3. Then pour in & stir the cream/milk.
4. Chill in the fridge, good up to a week.

MAPLE SYRUP OG & TASTE-A-LIKE

INGREDIENTS

AUTHENTIC SYRUP

1 five gallon bucket

(often a 40:1 ratio so 5 gallons creates 0.125 cups or 16 oz)

TASTE-A-LIKE

1 cup water, 2 cups brown sugar, 1 cup white sugar, 1 tbsp maple extract, 1 tsp vanilla extract

INSTRUCTIONS

1. In the late winter/early spring tap into your maple trees by drilling(5/16th bit) in 1 ½ inch at a slight upwards slant. Have tubes leading to 5 gall buckets. Collect every 2-3 days because sap can spoil.
2. Bring all the sap in a very large pot to a simmering boil, remove any initial foam and boil it down until it is slightly tinted yellow. Strain through mesh & store in an airtight container to freeze smaller batches.
3. Thaw/or skip freezing and boil into syrup. By heating the solution to 7 degrees over boiling point (changes based on elevation). But averages about 215/220. So using a candy thermometer get to 222. Then immediately remove from heat, strain if desired. And store in an airtight container in fridge 6 months, or freeze (good indefinitely).

1. Taste-a-like: simmer in medium pot until sugar ingredients are dissolved, reach 220 & remove from heat, store in airtight container in fridge.

HOMEMADE CHOCOLATE

WHITE CHOCOLATE

INGREDIENTS

¼ cup coconut oil (or butter)

5 tbsp milk powder

1/8 cup powdered sugar

INSTRUCTIONS

1. In a small sauce pan, melt coconut oil in the bowl on low Then sift powdered sugar until thoroughly mixed with no lumps until dissolved. Sift in milk powder, stir until combined.

2. Remove from heat, pour into molds (or piping bag method for chips). Cool in fridge to harden (~1-2 hrs).

MILK CHOCOLATE

INGREDIENTS

½ cup coconut oil (or cocoa butter)

3 tbsp milk powder

1/3 cup cocoa powder

¾ cup powdered sugar (or other sweetner)

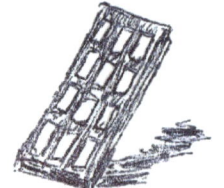

INSTRUCTIONS

1. Melt coconut oil in small sauce pan, then stir in cocoa powder, add in the milk powder whisking until fully combined. (low-medium heat)

2. Once all ingredients are combined, remove from heat but stir for 5-10 minutes after.

3. Pour into mold, or pipping bag onto wax paper (to make chips shape). Allow to cool to room temp then place in the fridge to harden.

SEMISWEET

INGREDIENTS

1/3 cup coconut oil or butter

2/3 cup honey

1 tsp vanilla extract

1 cup cocoa powder sifted

INSTRUCTIONS

1. Pregrease a loaf pan with coconut oil.

2. In a small saucepan melt coconut oil on low heat. Once melted add honey and vanilla.

3. Bring to a boil stir constantly for about 2 minutes then immediately remove from heat, whisk in cocoa powder until smooth. Pour into mold and smooth the top. Cool in fridge or freezer. Cut into chunks/shave.

DARK CHOCOLATE

INGREDIENTS

1:1 ratio of coconut oil (or cocoa butter) to cocoa powder

INSTRUCTIONS

1. Melt coconut oil (cocoa butter), whisk in cocoa powder, and sprinkle in the salt at the end.

2. Remove from heat, pour into mold (or turn into chocolate chips). Put in fridge or freezer to harden.

GENERAL TIPS

To prevent burning, try to use a double broiler or one large pot with a small pot inside of it elevated by forks inside of the handles of both pots. Fill the larger pot with water halfway up the smaller pot, and follow recipe.

(Use ziplock or pipping bag until a wax paper drop little drops to create chip shape.)

NOTE: Coconut oil & Butter can melt at room temp, for a heartier/solid chocolate use cocoa butter/Shea butter.

JAM

WHITE CHOCOLATE

INGREDIENTS

- ¼ cup coconut oil (or butter)
- 5 tbsp milk powder
- 1/8 cup powdered sugar

INSTRUCTIONS

1. Place all ingredients into small saucepan, bring to a boil, then lower slightly so that it still bubbles. Stir/simmer for about 30 minutes until thickened (sugar thickens nicely once it reaches 220 degrees).

2. Remove any initial foam that forms at the top of the boiling jam.

3. Pour jam into clean jars or keep in the fridge for up to a month. You can also water bath the jars and store in your pantry for a year.

BLACKBERRY

INGREDIENTS

- 5 cups blackberries
- 1-2 cups sugar
- 1-2 tbsp lemon juice

With canning, *leave a ¼ inch headspace and water bath for 10 minutes. (Cover your jars with a minimum of 1 inch of water above the lid). If using large jars (>pint), you'll need to water bath longer 15-20 minutes.*

STRAWBERRY (6 CUPS)

INGREDIENTS

- 8 cups raw strawberries
- 3 ½ cup white sugar
- 4 tbsp lemon juice

TIPS: *For smoother jam, remove skins/seed by straining through a mesh strainer or a food mill about 10 minutes after simmering the fruit.*

Some berries are not as full of liquid so you must add water (such as currant or blueberries, water) I would add ¼ cup of water for every cup of fruit)

GRAPE

INGREDIENTS

- 3 cups grapes (concord is best)
- 1 cup water
- 2 tbsp lemon juice

NOTE: All fruit naturally have pectin in them, in their seeds/peels/cores. As long as you are cooking the whole fruit initially you have the needed pectin to thicken your jam. You can use store bought pectin for any of these recipes to thicken up faster.

ICING/FROSTING

CREAM CHEESE ICING

INGREDIENTS

- ¼ block cream cheese
- 1 tbsp unsalted butter
- 1 cup of powdered sugar.
- 1 tsp vanilla extract

INSTRUCTIONS

1. Get cream cheese/butter to room temperature.
2. Whisk cream cheese, butter, powdered sugar and vanilla extract in a small bowl and its ready to use!

ROYAL ICING

INGREDIENTS

- 3 egg whites
- 1 ¾ cup powdered sugar
- 1 tsp vanilla extract

INSTRUCTIONS

1. Beat egg whites on medium until very frothy.(about 1-2 minutes).
2. Lower speed of mixer to low, then slowly add in sugar, adding the vanilla extract last.
3. Divide icing as desired to color.

(Beat powder for pink, tumeric for orange, green macha for green, cocoa powder-brown, etc.)

Double Broiler

BUTTERCREAM

INGREDIENTS

- 3 cups powdered sugar
- 1 cup butter(softened)
- 1 tsp vanilla extract
- 1-2 tbsp whipping cream

INSTRUCTIONS

1. Use a mixer to whisk sugar and butter until blended, increasing to med-high and whisk until fluffy.
2. Add in whipping cream, then vanilla. (add more cream as needed for desired consistency)

GANACHE

INGREDIENTS

- 1 cup of semisweet chocolate
- 1 cup heavy whipping cream

INSTRUCTIONS

1. Use double broiler method, or a small saucepan to heat whip cream. Pour simmering cream over the chocolate (in heatsafe bowl). Cover/sit for 5 min.
2. Whisk until chocolate/cream combine.

BONE/VEGGIE/CHICKEN BROTH

• (Pressure can at 10 lbs pressure for 25 minutes for quart sized jars)

CHICKEN BROTH (8 CUPS)

INGREDIENTS

1 whole chicken **(or ~ 4-5 lbs worth of chicken)**

10-12 cups of water

1 onion, 1 bay leaf

2 carrots

2 celery ribs

1 tbsp salt

2 tbsp black pepper.

-1 tbsp parsley, 1 tbsp thyme, 2 cloves of garlic,

INSTRUCTIONS

Use a large pot for stove top or crock pot(use crock pot for 6-8 hours). Cut up the whole chicken into smaller pieces and of course remove the giblets inside the chicken. On stove top add the water & chicken, bring to med-high heat, skim off any foam that initally forms. Next add all the rest of the ingredients and simmer for the next 1-5 hours (flavor always gets better with more time). Remove meat/veggies (enjoy). Then strain the broth through cheesecloth. Cool this in the fridge overnight. Scrape off excess fat if desired, and freeze(6 mo) or use within 4 days in the fridge.

BONE BROTH

INGREDIENTS

5 lbs bones (beef/chicken, femur, oxtail, shortribs, etc).

2 carrots

1 onion

1 whole garlic

3 stalks celery

2 bay leaves

¼ cup black pepper

2 tbsp apple cider vinegar

12 cups water

INSTRUCTIONS

Use slow cookers for ease of work. Otherwise fill large pot on stovetop with water and bones, bring to a boil then immedietly lower to simmer for 20 minutes. Drain/rinse bones and place throughout cookie sheets, adding the veggies as well. Preheat to 450 degrees and roast for 25 minutes, flip, then roast another 20 minutes. Wash the original pot while it roasts. Once done, add all ingredients into pot and about 12 cups of water (or until everything is submerged). Bring to a boil then simmer/low for 8-24 hours (add water as needed). Strain, (use veggies/meats for meal), skim fat if desired after cooling. Freeze(6 mo) or use within 5 days in fridge.

VEGGIE

INGREDIENTS

1 tbsp olive oil, 1 yellow onion, 4 garlic cloves, 2 bay leaves, 2 tsp black pepper, ½ tsp salt, 12 cups of water, 1-gallon Ziplock of veggie scraps

INSTRUCTIONS

In a large pot, sauté the onion/garlic in the oil. Once browned, add the rest of the ingredients. Bring to a boil then simmer for about 1 hour (simmer longer for preferred taste or if it tastes watery). Strain ingredients out, and freeze, or store in fridge.

GENERAL CANNING TIPS

WATERBATH

High acid foods (Jams, Preserves, fruits, pickled vegetables, chutneys(spicy condiments), acidified tomatoes. ~BELOW NOTES are for pint size or smaller jars

GENERAL INSTRUCTIONS

1. Clean/sterilize jars with soap or by boiling in water.
2. Prepare your filling. Pour your filling into the clean jars, leave ¼ inch to rim.
3. Wipe the rims, place on the lid (finger tight), and place into a boiling & tall enough pot that 1-2 inches of water sits above the jars.
4. Boil the jars for the indicated time (based on your elevation, and the size of your jars.) Pull out, rest on towel for 24 hrs. Check seals/Store.

NOTE: Some fillings need to be hot packed/simmered in water before packing (ex. apples, fruit puree, pears, rhubarb, pickling brines).

PICKLING

Cucumbers, onions, garlic, carrots, zucchini, green beans, peppers

Process ~10-15 min

1. In a small saucepan create a brine (ensure you have enough acidity).

   Simple brine recipe (1:1 cup of water/vinegar, 1 pinch dill, 1 garlic clove, 1 pinch salt)
2. Pack in desired veggie, pour brine over.

WHOLE FRUIT

Peaches, citrus, cranberries, apples, pears, etc.

Process 8-10 min

1. Peel fruit/remove any cores, and pack into jars. Often harder fruit needs to be "Hot packed" ex. Applesauce. (Some fruit does better blanched ex. peaches)
2. Pour water, juice or syrup until fruit is covered.

   (syrup is made by stirring a 2:1 ratio of water to sugar)

PRESSURE CANNING	Low acid foods (Meat, chili, beans, corn, all veggies not pickled)
SOUPS	Prepare soup on stovetop. Pour into jars, **Process for 60 min in pints & 75 min. for quarts** (if containing meat-follow meat guidelines for canning), Know your elevation **11 psi for elevation of 2000 or less for dial gauge pressure canning.**
MEAT	Proces,s if containing seafood, for at least 100 minutes. Process chicken for 75 minutes (for pints).
VEGGIES	Blanch veggies (add to boiling water for about 5 minutes and remove). Pack jars, pour boiling water to fill jar. Process 75 min. for pints, 90 min. for quarts

Refer to official guidelines for specific fruits/veggies as above tips are a general explanation

GENERAL DEHYDRATION TIPS

	INGREDIENTS	INSTRUCTIONS
HERBS	Leaf herbs (mint, basil, etc) can burn easily *NOTE: Root herbs (thicker & require 6-8 hours)*	**Oven:** Remove leafs from stems, rinse with cold water and blot dry with a paper towel. Scatter in a single layer on a cookie sheet, bake at lowest setting with the oven cracked (not on gas ovens- not safe). Bake ~1 hr. **Dehydrator:** Set at 95-115 degrees for 1-5 hours depending on the herb/thickenss.
VEGGIES	Onions, celery, garlic, corn, beets, carrots, etc.	**Oven:** Thinly slice then blanch veggies in boiling water 3 min, strain then dehydrate lowest temp for 4-6 hrs **Dehydrator:** Set at 140 degrees. Ranges 4-10 hrs. *(TIP: for seasoning-use a coffee grinder to turn into a powder.)*
FRUIT	**Fruit of choice** (apples, tomatoes, etc) (Use lemon juice to retain colors on fruits like apples/bananas)	**Oven:** Always rinse all fruit, Peel/core if necessary (ex, tomatoes/apples). Cut into thin slices if applicable. Steam/blanch to help coloring. Optionally: sprinkle with sugar. Bake lowest setting ~4-8 hrs. **Dehydrator:** Set at 135-140 for 12-24 hrs (may take even more if fruit has high water content)
LIQUIDS	Starches, Juices, Broths, fruit leathers TIP: staple or paper clip edges of parchment to create a powder tray	**Oven:** Use a cookie sheet with tall enough edges, don't use tinfoil as a liner (only silicone or parchment). 6-10 hrs, rotating shelves a few hrs in. **Dehydrator:** Set to 130-150 for about 8 hrs
MEAT (Stores Room temp 1-2 mo or freeze for a year.)	**Lean meat** Jerky marinade: (4 tbsp soy sauce, 4 tbsp Worcestershire, 2 tbsp lq. Smoke, 1 tbsp ketchup, ½ tsp salt, ¼ tsp pepper, ¼ tsp garlic, ¼ tsp onion, 1 lb meat)	**Oven:** Freeze meat before cutting thin slices (1/8 inch) or ground meat out of a jerky gun. Marinate meat in desired cure for 8-12 hrs in the fridge. Layer on cookie sheet, use a grate for more even cooking. Bake 8-12 hours lowest temp, leave oven cracked (no gas ovens) **Dehydrator:** Set at 165 for 3 hrs & 145 for ~4 more hrs. *TIP: Cut meat against the grain for easier chewing*

MEAT PRESERVATION TIPS

	INGREDIENTS/ EQUIPMENT	INSTRUCTIONS
COLD SMOKING	Enclosed smoker kept at 50-68°F/10-20°C, 65-80% humidity *Properly cured meat will reduce in weight by 20-30%.*	Fresh lean Meat is properly weighed then cured and hung in an enclosure from 1 day up to 6 weeks. (Usually 1 day per pound of meat). Requires flavorful hardwoods ex. Apple or cherry. (No using bitter trees like softwoods ex. Pines/firs or toxic trees ex. walnut/sassafras). You need a smoker or smoke machine. The meat will require "rests" in the fridge every 4-8 hrs. People often cold-smoke in the winter for best results. Weigh your meat & determine if properly cured. This is a long process & requires equipment, but it's still interesting to learn about, and creates flavorful meats.
HOT SMOKING **(80-145 DEGREES)**	**Salmon "wet" brine** 4 cups water, ½ c white sugar and brown sugar, 1/3 cup salt, 1 lemon zest	Using fresh salmon brine 8-12 hr in the fridge then **drain on a rack/cookie sheet in fridge another 8-12 hrs(this will form a pellicle).** Hot smoke 3-4 hrs at 145 degrees.
	Bacon wet Brine 6 cups water, 1 c white sugar & brown sugar, 2 tsp prague powder, 1 c salt, 1 bay leave, 1 tbsp peppercorns.	Fresh pork belly for Bacon wet brines 7 days in fridge (flip in solution every other day). For HOT smoking. Get the grill/smoker to 80-120 degrees. Smoke for 3 hours, rotate the pork, continue smoking another 2-3 hrs until internal temp reaches 160. **Now the meat has cured, but it still requires cooking/frying.** (Stores 1 week in fridge, 2 months in freezer, VS-6 months in freezer)
	Bacon Dry Cure/Brine ¼ cup salt, ¼ cup brown sugar, 1 tsp prague powder	Fresh Pork belly, rub every surface with cure (use coffee grinder for easier powder texture) cure in fridge 5 days, rub back in any leaking liquid, cure another 5 days. Then either cold smoke or hot smoke.

Dry salt curing/brines often follows a 2% rule (2 g of salt per 100 g of meat). For weeks-up to a year. (cold smoked bacon, hot smoked Salami, etc). **Wet salt brines or cures**-1% rule in submerging meat in salty brine for 1-6 weeks before hot smoking it.(turkey, fish, bacon)

FREEZING

Regular ziplock (Z)

Vs.

Vacuum sealed (VS)

Raw meat varies: Seafood if VS lasts 2 years but 3 months in a Z.

Chicken, red meats if VS lasts 2-3 years, 3-12 months If in Z

Cooked meats varies but generally VS is good up to 6 months. 1-3 months if in container/Ziplock.

NOTE: All cooked meats should be tossed after ~4 days in the fridge.

SUBSTITUTING MADE EASY

1 EGG	1 tbsp chia seeds + 3 tbsp water OR 2 tbsp water + 2 tsp baking powder + 1 tsp oil	**BROWN SUGAR**	1:1-2tsp molasses+1 cup white sugar
BUTTER/OILS	Often 1:1 replacement with coconut oil or ¾ cup olive/veggie oil: 1 If low on butter, replace it by half with applesauce/banana/avocado	**MILK/NON DAIRY (SEE OATMILK)**	Oatmilk 1:1 Half&half watered down. Heavy cream watered down.
1 TSP BAKING POWDER	¼ tsp baking soda + 1 ½ tsp vinegar (don't overmix) OR 1 tsp baking soda + 1 tsp cream of tartar OR 2 egg whites whipped	**OATMILK**	1 cup oats, 4-6 cups filtered water, 1 tsp vanilla extract. (blend for 30 sec., then strain through cheesecloth-no squeezing-good 4 5 days)
1 CUP SUGAR	1:3/4 cup maple syrup/ or honey OR 1: 1 1/3 cup molasses OR Agave/dates (pureed) 1:1 1: 1 tsp stevia 1: ½ cup monkfruit ~You can also use fruit puree as a replacement but will need to decrease liquid in recipe too	**SOUR CREAM** **POWDERED SUGAR**	Made with 1 cup heavy cream, 2 tsp lemon juice ¼ cup milk. Mix, cover with a cover filter/cloth and leave out overnight. 1:1 cup sugar(blended)+1tsbp starch (corn or potato, etc.)

FOOD COLORING OR DYE ALTERNATIVES

Pink/Red: beets/beet powder, cranberries, strawberries, pomegranates

Blue: red cabbage & baking soda or spirulina

Orange: sweet potato carrot powder/juice

Yellow: turmeric powder

Green: Matcha powder, spinach powder

Purple: red cabbage or blueberries

Black: blackberries, black cacao powder

Brown: coffee, cinnamon, cocoa powder

Sour cream, plain yogurt, mayo, ricotta cheese, cottage cheese, and cream cheese are often interchangeable with baking/cooking.

TIPS ON COOKING FROM AN ACTIVE HUNTING, FISHING & FRUGAL FAMILY

We eat the meat from deer and elk year round, serve up the fish we catch when we can and try to use all the perishable food we buy one way or another to save money and cut the waste. Deer can be "gamey" and I use to hate it! Now I will soak in buttermilk the night before, cook with stronger acidity and with the style of low and slow to help. You can also try brining it with salty water to draw out the gamey flavor/excess blood.

I like to keep a Ziplock of meat scraps(undesirable trimmings) and veggie scraps (onions skins, peels, stems, pulp, etc) in the freezer then once it fills up it gets turned into stock or broth. I'm lucky enough to have chickens working year round to turn other food scraps into delicious and healthy eggs as well as compost material. (did you know chickens can eat meat? It helps provide them that extra needed protein in the winter months)

When I make bread or use sourdough I always try to wipe off stirring utensils/dump containers as much as possible via a paper towel/cloth before washing in the sink because I've learned the hard way it can turn into a nice plaster and clog your pipes (good thing I married a plumber).

When cooking with cast iron or stainless steel wait for it to get hot before adding in your ingredients! I do a butter test, in which I add a pat of butter and once it has fully melted it's most likely ready to cook on. For meat/eggs I cook between low and medium and don't stir until that bottom side has started to change color. Doing so helps to keep it from burning or sticking. Cast iron care is simple. Don't use soap! While the pan is hot, rub off food scraps, rinse with water, pat dry and then lightly oil while still warm (reheat on low if it needs cleaning/oiling and has cooled off.)

Use your resources, Use your freezer, if you have a vaccum sealer things last longer, plant a small raised bed in your yard, or keep a few herbs in a window. Buy in bulk when possible, things like 5 gallon buckets with sealable lids, mason jars with lids can keep a lot of pantry goods from spoiling and you get more bang for your buck.

If you can hunt, fish, forage do it. Check out books on those topics. You can barter with neighbors and friends that may grow things you don't. (My neighbor has multiple fruit trees and a lot of chickens). Seek out farmer markets for fresh produce,

Whenever I cook, I recommend using the raw ingredient because it's fresh and, in my opinion, adds more flavor. (For example, use minced garlic over garlic powder). However, use what you got when you've got it! See my replacement page for when you're cooking and need an alternative because it's out of stock in your pantry!

I am a lover of keeping down the grocery bill so I work with what I've got. Another way we cut down on costs is to have a variety of reusable equipment! Silicone mats for cookie sheets instead of rolls of parchment paper. Reusable zip locks (I do not use these for raw meat-only freezer bags for that). Clothe covers for bread rising or for keeping food covered instead of tinfoil or saran wrap. Beeswax cloth wraps instead of plastic wraps. It might initially be an investment, but it pays for itself especially when you're making meals and snacks for a big family.

Whether you are reading this book just for meals, for cutting out unnecessary and oftentimes unhealthy ingredients, or saving money, I hope it gives you the knowledge and confidence to cook more from scratch and enjoying the process that got you to the end product.

www.ingramcontent.com/pod-product-compliance
Lightning Source LLC
Chambersburg PA
CBHW042022150426
43198CB00002B/41